Your Early Childhood Practicum and Student Teaching Experience

Guidelines for Success

Carroll Tyminski
Elizabethtown College

PEARSON

Merrill
Prentice Hall

Upper Saddle River, New Jersey
Columbus, Ohio

Library of Congress Cataloging in Publication Data

Tyminski, Carroll.
   Your early childhood practicum and student teaching experience :
guidelines for success / Carroll Tyminski.
     p. cm.
  ISBN 0-13-048817-8
  1. Student teaching--United States.   2. Preschool teachers--Training of--United States.
3. Primary school teachers--Training of--United States.   I. Title.
  LB2157.U5T96 2006
  370'.71'1--dc22

                    2005014011

Vice President and Executive Publisher: Jeffery W. Johnston
Publisher: Kevin M. Davis
Editor: Julie Peters
Editorial Assistant: Michelle Girgis
Production Editor: Sheryl Glicker Langner
Production Coordination: Mike Remillard, Pine Tree Composition

Design Coordinator: Diane C. Lorenzo
Cover Design: Tom Borah
Cover Image: Corbis
Photo Coordinator: Valerie Schultz
Production Manager: Laura Messerly
Director of Marketing: Ann Castel Davis
Marketing Manager: Autumn Purdy
Marketing Coordinator: Amy Judd

This book was set in Palatino Light by Pine Tree Composition. It was printed and bound by R. R. Donnelly & Sons Company. The cover was printed by R. R. Donnelly & Sons Company.

Photo Credits: Anne Vega/Merrill, pp. 1, 8, 29, 55, 87, 107, 154; Anthony Magnacca/Merrill, pp. 11, 19, 23, 39, 98, 118, 141; Kathy Kirtland/Merrill, p. 37; Barbara Schwartz/Merrill, p. 51; Scott Cunningham/Merrill, pp. 71, 74, 76, 114, 125, 144, 163, 171; David Mager/Pearson Learning Photo Sudio, pp. 147, 161; Tim Cairns/Merrill, p. 157.

Pearson Prentice Hall™ is a trademark of Pearson Education, Inc.
Pearson® is a registered trademark of Pearson plc
Prentice Hall® is a registered trademark of Pearson Education, Inc.
Merrill® is a registered trademark of Pearson Education, Inc.

Pearson Education Ltd.
Pearson Education Singapore, Pte. Ltd
Pearson Education, Canada, Ltd
Pearson Education–Japan

Pearson Education Australia Pty, Limited
Pearson Education North Asia Ltd
Pearson Educación de Mexico, S.A. de C.V.
Pearson Education Malaysia, Pte. Ltd

10 9 8 7 6 5 4
ISBN: 0-13-048817-8

Your Early Childhood Practicum and Student Teaching Experience: Guidelines for Success is designed for students who are assuming the responsibilities of teaching young children while receiving guidance and supervision. Students may be taking part in a variety of student teaching experiences. These may include capstone courses for one-year certificate programs and for associate degree programs, practicum experiences in a community college setting, as well as traditional early childhood programs in a four-year university setting. This text offers both theory and practical application to guide each student to a successful conclusion of the practicum and student teaching experience.

The author has mentored and supervised countless preservice teachers over the years. Students' recurring questions and comments became the impetus for this text. Thus, the need for a reality-based guide to shepherd students through this important experience became readily apparent.

FEATURES OF TEXT

This text provides an opportunity for present and future early childhood preservice teachers to benefit from the experiences of those who have recently gone before them. Each chapter begins with *Voices of Reality*, quotes from recent early childhood student teachers. The author believes it is important for students to reflect on their experiences and to share their stories with others. Relatively little research has been reported concerning the student teaching experience itself. Therefore, the anecdotal comments, quotes, and eclectic wisdom of early childhood student teachers and teacher educators have been included as valuable teaching and learning tools.

In addition, this text is a reference containing research-based, practical advice on such topics as developmentally appropriate practices and teacher competencies. Special care has been taken to include a broad range of early childhood experiences from birth through age 8. It contains special emphasis on being a professional as well as the importance of ethics.

The text guides students from the early days of preparing to begin the practicum right through the final days of leaving the practicum as well as everything in between. The author provides real-life examples in each chapter as an effective way to help students understand how to apply the suggestions given. Activities are suggested at the end of each chapter to encourage student reflection and application of the information.

Several areas receive particular attention in this text. For example, communication is emphasized as an important skill for teachers. There is an overview of strategies and key questions to improve communication with both children and adults.

Focus on Culture and Human Diversity

The education of children with special needs is also an essential component of this text due to the increasing demand for inclusionary practice in early childhood programs. In addition, a recurring theme throughout the text is the importance of culture and human diversity. There is a focus on examining cultural assumptions. Students are asked to think about those aspects of their cultural experience that might influence their interactions with children and adults. Important issues related to culture and families are included, and there are questions for reflection in order to help students develop cultural competency.

FORMAT AND CHAPTER SEQUENCE

Each chapter begins with a quotation and a brief discussion that relates to the particular topic being emphasized. This is followed by a section called *Voices of Reality: Student Teachers Speak* containing quotations from recent student teachers related to the topic. Chapter content is presented next. Visuals are included in each chapter to encourage students' reflection and to provide suggestions for practical application of material. Chapters end with *Voices of Reality: Student Teachers Speak.* This section contains quotations to wrap up the information presented with student teachers' relevant thoughts on each subject. Each chapter concludes with a section called *Activities for Reflection and Action* that encourages readers to reflect on and/or implement the information.

Chapter 1, "Preparing to Begin Student Teaching," includes many different topics, such as making a good first impression, examination of personal assumptions and beliefs, initial meetings, personal preparations, and development of a support system. Real-life examples are provided to help students understand how to apply the suggestions given.

Chapter 2, "Becoming a Professional," includes such topics as what it means to become a professional, ethical guidelines and professional standards, confidentiality, sources for professional decision making, and professional growth as a team member. This chapter focuses on ethics as a foundation for being a professional.

Chapter 3, "Establishing Effective Professional Relationships," includes the topics of establishing positive relationships with your cooperating teacher and college supervisor, developing effective communication skills, and stages of student teaching. Practical suggestions are provided to encourage dialogue.

Chapter 4, "Guiding Young Children in the Classroom," contains topics such as discipline and guidance, guidance strategies, class meetings, additional behavior management techniques, and real-life ethical dilemmas. This chapter provides an in-depth look at the guidance function as essential to the student teacher's success in the classroom.

Chapter 5, "Classroom Management: Environments and Routines," includes topics related to physical space, emotional climate, safety, classroom routines, time management, and transitions. This chapter addresses the concept of meeting children's needs through the physical environment.

Chapter 6, "Observations and Evaluations of Student Teaching," includes topics related to making the most of the observation/evaluation process. It includes topics such as purposes and format of observations, receiving criticism, reflective journaling, portfolios, state standards, certification, and praxis tests.

Chapter 7, "Assessment of Young Children," includes topics such as the purposes of assessment, standards, examples of formal and informal assessment, types of authentic assessments, and alternative assessment. Examples and formats for data collection are included as well as the linkage between assessment and teaching practice.

Chapter 8, "Supportive Instruction," includes topics such as relating instruction to young children's ways of knowing, multiple intelligences, applied concepts of developmentally appropriate practice, integrated curriculum, the project approach, and technology. Important concepts are included related to curriculum and how children learn.

Chapter 9, "Understanding Diverse Communities and Interacting with Children's Families," begins with a discussion of changing cultural demographics. It includes topics such as breaking down cultural barriers, developing positive home–school relationships, creating culture-friendly classrooms, parent conferences, and nonverbal cultural codes. Practical suggestions are provided as well as questions for students' reflection on their own culture and experience with diversity.

Chapter 10, "Completion of Student Teaching: Looking Ahead," gives practical suggestions for leaving your student teaching practicum, the final evaluation of the student teaching experience, and tips for planning ahead in the areas of networking, resume writing, applications, and interviews.

USING THE TEXT

Instructors are encouraged to select the chapters most relevant to the needs of their particular students. For example, if students are already familiar with their practicum site, then portions of the first chapter may be omitted or skimmed. If students already have employment in child care settings, then portions of the last chapter may be omitted.

SUPPLEMENTARY MATERIALS

Two supplementary products have been created to support this text. The *Instructor's Manual and Test Bank* includes instructional tips and assessment items. Contact your Prentice Hall representative to learn how to download this resource from a secure online site. The Companion Website provides practice self-assessments for students and a Syllabus Manager for instructors. It can be accessed a **www.prehall.com/tyminski.** See page vii of this text for additional information.

ACKNOWLEDGMENTS

I would like to acknowledge the contribution of my late mother, Erdene B. Rountree. Without her love, her support, and her regular phone calls to ask, "How is that book coming along?" this text might not have been completed.

I also wish to express appreciation to the many students and cooperating teachers who offered their support and contributed in one way or another to this text. Special recognition goes to the following: Jamie Brandt, Lauren Crane, Angie DePauli, Adam Dively, Jennifer Dotson, Amanda Fisher, Megan Hilperts, Elisabeth Kimmel, Diane LaMonica, Melissa Lenhert, Amanda Myers, Beth Nickle, Megan Tyson, and Krista Unger.

Thank you, also, to those who reviewed this text and provided valuable comments: Jodelle Austin, University of Maine; Alice Beyrent, Hesser College; Toni Campbell, San Jose State University; Phyllis Cuevas, McNeese State University; Georgianna Duarte, University of Texas–Brownsville; Patricia Hofbauer, Northwest State Community College; Diane Kubetz, College of DuPage; LeAnna Manna, Villa Maria College; Anita McLeod, Presbyterian College; Jean C. Murphy, Chicago State University; Sharon Seidman, California State University–Fullerton; and Linda Anderson Welsh, Austin Community College.

DISCOVER THE COMPANION WEBSITE ACCOMPANYING THIS BOOK

THE PRENTICE HALL COMPANION WEBSITE: A VIRTUAL LEARNING ENVIRONMENT

Technology is a constantly growing and changing aspect of our field that is creating a need for content and resources. To address this emerging need, Prentice Hall has developed an online learning environment for students and professors alike—Companion Websites—to support our textbooks.
In creating a Companion Website, our goal is to build on and enhance what the textbook already offers. For this reason, the content for each user-friendly website is organized by topic and provides the professor and student with a variety of meaningful resources. Common features of a Companion Website include:

FOR THE PROFESSOR

Every Companion Website integrates *Syllabus Manager*™, an online syllabus creation and management utility.

- *Syllabus Manager*™ provides you, the instructor, with an easy, step-by-step process to create and revise syllabi, with direct links into Companion Website and other online content without having to learn HTML.
- Students may logon to your syllabus during any study session. All they need to know is the web address for the Companion Website and the password you've assigned to your syllabus.
- After you have created a syllabus using *Syllabus Manager*™, students may enter the syllabus for their course section from any point in the Companion Website.
- Clicking on a date, the student is shown the list of activities for the assignment. The activities for each assignment are linked directly to actual content, saving time for students.
- Adding assignments consists of clicking on the desired due date, then filling in the details of the assignment name of the assignment, instructions, and whether it is a one-time or repeating assignment.
- In addition, links to other activities can be created easily. If the activity is online, a URL can be entered in the space provided, and it will be linked automatically in the final syllabus.

- Your completed syllabus is hosted on our servers, allowing convenient updates from any computer on the Internet. Changes you make to your syllabus are immediately available to your students at their next logon.

FOR THE STUDENT

- *Self-Assessment*—Ten multiple-choice assessment items provide students with the opportunity to take a practice quiz to check their understanding.
- *Cases*—A mini-case for each chapter includes a narrative description of a classroom dilemma or conflict requiring decision-making.
- *Web Destinations*—lists significant and up-to-date sites to support your student teaching experience.
- *Message Board*—serves as a virtual bulletin board to post—or respond to—questions or comments to/from a national audience.
- *ECE Resources*—A link to Merrill Education's *Early Childhood Education Resources* Website, containing a wealth of resources, such as timely articles, school websites, observation tools, and much more.

BRIEF CONTENTS

EDUCATOR LEARNING CENTER: AN INVALUABLE ONLINE RESOURCE

Merrill Education and the Association for Supervision and Curriculum Development (ASCD) invite you to take advantage of a new online resource, one that provides access to the top research and proven strategies associated with ASCD and Merrill the Educator Learning Center. At *www.educatorlearningcenter.com,* you will find resources that will enhance your students understanding of course topics and of current educational issues, in addition to being invaluable for further research.

HOW THE EDUCATOR LEARNING CENTER WILL HELP YOUR STUDENTS BECOME BETTER TEACHERS

With the combined resources of Merrill Education and ASCD, you and your students will find a wealth of tools and materials to better prepare them for the classroom.

Research

- More than 600 articles from the ASCD journal *Educational Leadership* discuss everyday issues faced by practicing teachers.
- A direct link on the site to Research Navigator™ gives students access to many of the leading education journals, as well as extensive content detailing the research process.
- Excerpts from Merrill Education texts give your students insights on important topics of instructional methods, diverse populations, assessment, classroom management, technology, and refining classroom practice.

Classroom Practice

- Hundreds of lesson plans and teaching strategies are categorized by content area and age range.
- Case studies and classroom video footage provide virtual field experience for student reflection.
- Computer simulations and other electronic tools keep your students abreast of today's classrooms and current technologies.

LOOK INTO THE VALUE OF EDUCATOR LEARNING CENTER YOURSELF

A four-month subscription to Educator Learning Center is $25 but is *FREE* when packaged with any Merrill Education text. In order for your students to have access to this site, you must use this special value-pack ISBN number *WHEN* placing your textbook order with the bookstore: 0-13-169981-4. Your students will then receive a copy of the text packaged with a free ASCD pincode. To preview the value of this website to you and your students, please go to *www.educatorlearningcenter.com* and click on Demo.

CONTENTS

Note: Every effort has been made to provide accurate and current Internet information in this book. However, the Internet and information posted on it are consistently changing, and it is inevitable that some of the Internet addresses listed in this textbook will change.

CHAPTER 1

Preparing to Begin Student Teaching

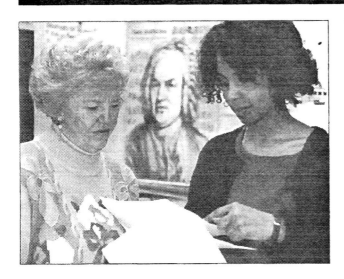

"Only the brave should teach. Only those who love the young should teach. Teaching is a vocation. It is as sacred as priesthood, as innate as desire, as inescapable as the genius which compels a great artist. If he has not the concern for humanity, the love of living creatures, the vision of the priest and the artist, he must not teach."

Pearl S. Buck

Pearl S. Buck's characterization of teaching as a sacred vocation may sound somewhat dramatic. It contains, however, basic elements central to successful preservice teaching. Many veteran teachers agree that the best teachers have a passion for teaching that may be compared to a sacred calling. They have an intense desire to teach. They may describe it as a wish to make the world a better place or to make a difference in human lives—one child at a time. They have the courage to believe that *all* children can learn regardless of their diverse cultural backgrounds and abilities. They also have a sincere love of the young as indicated by the respect, dignity, and concern that they show each child.

Successful students find that they are embarking upon a career that is a life choice, not a nine-to-five job. They think about "their" children after they leave school; they become consumed with how to improve each child's well-being in a holistic sense. They focus on social, emotional, and physical concerns as well as academic improvement. In other words, they exhibit what Pearl Buck describes as a passionate, visionary concern and love for living creatures.

❖ FINAL PREPARATIONS FOR DAY ONE

Now that your passion, vision, and love for children have been acknowledged, how do you prepare to begin this all-important student teaching

Voices of Reality: Student Teachers Speak

I am bubbling with excitement. The possibilities for touching and helping to shape these lives are endless; and to think that I may have a hand in this impact fills me with warmth from head to toe.

Karla S.

I'm terrified of failure. I'm afraid that I won't be able to balance being friendly and firm, and the students won't like me. What if my lessons are all a flop? What if I can't get the kids to understand and make a/the connection?

Luke B.

I am mostly afraid that I will not be adequately prepared for the job that lays ahead of me. That I will not be able to be a successful student teacher. That I will fail.

Meisha T.

I'm excited to get started. Concerned about not having control of the class, fitting in at the school, working with my co-op. I'm just a bit nervous (but again excited).

Jamal D.

I met my co-op. She gave me a building tour and introduced me to the principal, and I called today to remind her I'm starting tomorrow. . . . I know it will be successful.

Keeley N.

experience? What are your concerns? What excites you as you anticipate your first days and weeks?

After an informational meeting for students who were beginning their practicum or their student teaching the next day, the early childhood student teachers voluntarily shared their innermost feelings in a small group setting. You may be a little surprised by their candor. Some expressed severe self-doubts while others exuded confidence. You may find yourself somewhere in between these two extremes.

In any event, most students approach a practicum or a student teaching experience with a mixture of nervousness and excitement. This is normal. Sometimes it is helpful to realize that you are not alone as your emotions swing among enthusiasm, excitement, frustration, and anxiety. You may recognize the feelings of butterflies in your stomach, restless periods of sleep, loss of appetite, or any combination of these. Anytime you begin a new experience with uncertain outcomes, you may have mixed feelings. However, there are several steps you can take to lessen your uneasiness and increase your chances of success before you begin. Generally speaking, the student teaching practicum is a rewarding, positive experience for everyone involved.

❖ TERMINOLOGY OF STUDENT TEACHING

Depending on geographical area, custom, and/or the characteristics of a particular educational program, the terms used to describe student teaching and the key people involved may vary greatly. Student teaching may be referred to as a practicum, a professional internship, or a field experience. You may have chosen the setting of your student teaching practicum or you may have been assigned a location unfamiliar to you. Regardless of these differences, there are generally three key people involved in the experience.

[Note: For the sake of simplicity and consistency, gender references, when used at all, will be female. Choice of gender in no way implies bias related to role or position of authority.]

- **Cooperating teacher:** This person is sometimes referred to as a co-op, the lead teacher, the supervising teacher, the master teacher, or the clinical teacher. She will supervise work, model good teaching practices, and mentor your professional growth on a daily basis.
- **Supervisor:** You may be assigned to a supervisor. This person is sometimes referred to as the college/university supervisor, a teacher trainer, the off-campus supervisor, the practicum instructor, or the clinical supervisor. She will make regular visits and serve as a mentor and resource to both you and your cooperating teacher.
- **Student teacher:** As a student teacher, you may sometimes be referred to as an intern or an apprentice. You will be experiencing a consecutive period of supervised planning and teaching during which you assume increasing responsibilities. This experience may be part of a course in which you are currently enrolled or it may be the culminating experience undertaken after the completion of your education coursework.

Regardless of these differences, you have a wonderful opportunity to influence the lives of children and to embark upon a personal journey of growth.

❖ MAKING A GOOD FIRST IMPRESSION

You have completed all your prerequisites, and now you have the opportunity to shine as you polish your professional skills. You want to get off on the right foot by making a good first impression.

Develop Knowledge Base

You have been assigned a child development center or a school for your student teaching experience. Unless you are already quite familiar with the setting for your practicum, consider doing some homework before you begin

Demographics refers to vital and social data such as racial and ethnic populations and numbers of students receiving special education services. It may also include characteristics that classify people by age, gender, and income.

your student teaching. Get on the Internet and try to locate information about your center or school. Many child development centers and public or private schools have their own Web sites. If your assigned location is part of a public school system, you can go directly to your state's Department of Education site and locate your district and specific school. State Web sites include such information as enrollment, enrollment stability, class size, programs available, teacher absenteeism, and assessment results. If your school is either a private facility or a center specifically for infants and preschoolers, you may be able to obtain informational booklets printed for prospective students and their families. You will make a better first impression with your cooperating teacher and school administration if you are knowledgeable about the school itself, its mission, and its **demographics.**

❖ EXAMINATION OF PERSONAL ASSUMPTIONS AND BELIEFS

Pluralistic societies may be described as those in which diverse cultural groups maintain their unique identities as they coexist.

Be aware of your own reactions to the diversity or apparent lack of diversity you encounter in your placement. We may assume that everyone's teacher education curriculum has included elements of multiculturalism and diversity training. As students in a **pluralistic society,** you have been taught to avoid stereotypes of particular socioeconomic, racial, or ethnic groups.

Nevertheless, it may be helpful to reflect once again on your personal expectations. You pass through the local neighborhoods on your way to your practicum each day. Do you have preconceptions based on your impressions that the neighborhoods apparently contain children of high-income families or children of impoverished families or children of a particular racial or ethnic background? Our own culture is so entwined in every aspect of our existence that "it becomes the invisible script that directs our personal lives" (Hollins, 1995, p. 72). You may strongly believe that you harbor no stereotypes, but "most teachers, though unknowingly, discriminate against culturally different students by lacking the sensitivity, knowledge, and skills necessary to teach them properly" (Diller & Moule, 2005, p. 2). Whether you are a member of a minority culture or a member of the white, middle-class majority, you may be unaware of your own biases that can be inadvertently communicated to children and co-workers.

Reflective Inquiry to Raise Awareness and Reduce Harmful Assumptions

Accordingly, as you begin your early childhood practicum, you may consider several topics for ongoing reflective inquiry. These reflections may become particularly significant if your own cultural heritage differs from that of your

Questions for Self-Reflection

1. What are my own beliefs about young children from particular cultural groups?
2. What are my assumptions about young children from particular socioeconomic groups?
3. What beliefs do I have about instruction that may reflect my own biases concerning cultural values?
4. What similarities and differences do I believe exist between social interaction in the classroom and social interaction in the children's home environments?
5. What significant experiences do I believe young children may bring to the classroom?
6. How much do I know about the cultural values, beliefs, and practices in the homes of my young children?
7. How much do I know about political and/or social influences within the local community that may affect interactions with the families of my young children? (Hollins, 1995)

children. The likelihood of this cultural diversity increases as our nation continues to experience demographic changes.

Part of your lifelong professional growth as a teacher involves developing the ability to be objective, empathetic, and sensitive in your responses to the needs of young children and their families. Few, if any, of your children will have your exact family background. You will strive for shared understanding. This is not an easy task. At one time or another you may be communicating with children and families of widely diverse backgrounds including but not limited to the following: African American families, Asian American families, Native American families, single teenage parent families, stepfamilies, grandparents as substitute parents, families with special needs children, and gay and lesbian families. No one can expect you to have perfected your communication skills by the time you become a certified teacher. You may feel uncertain at times. Nevertheless, your humility, honesty, flexibility, energy, and dedicated advocacy for young children and their families will enable you to be perceived as a caring teacher. As the famous quote by an unknown author says, "No one cares how much you know until they know how much you care."

Potential for Cultural Misconceptions

You may or may not be surprised to learn that data collected by the National Education Association (NEA) indicates that over 90% of teachers in the United States are white, and the majority of these come from middle-class backgrounds (Fuller, 2001). At the same time, the numbers of children who are from minority backgrounds are increasing rapidly. In some states, California for example, the majority of the children in school programs are from cultural minority groups (Fuller, 2001). The population of immigrant children in our schools is also increasing rapidly; reports indicate that over three million children are considered English-language learners. Many of these children and their families experience "struggles with [both] a new culture and a new language" (Miller & Endo, 2004, p. 786).

With so many differences between the culture of the teachers and the culture of the children, the potential exists for misconceptions to develop between schools and families. In fact, "the student's culture is often in conflict with the culture in the school" (Ducette, Sewell, & Shapiro, 1996, p. 363). This cultural mismatch may have a negative impact on children from particular cultural groups that are historically underserved in our public school systems (Hollins, 1995). Therefore, curricular and instructional interventions may be necessary in order to legitimize the connections between traditional learning in the schools and learning in the children's home and community environments (McCarty, Lynch, Wallace, & Benally, 1991; Moll, 1986). We know that "children learn and grow best in schools where parents and teachers understand one another, share similar, visions, and collaborate on guiding children" (Grant & Gomez, 2001, p. 130). Therefore, suggestions for preventing misconceptions and increasing understanding will be discussed later in the text.

❖ INITIAL MEETINGS

Being the conscientious student that you are, you have done your homework concerning the demographics of your practicum or student teaching site. You have addressed your own cultural assumptions and beliefs regarding your children and their families. Now, have you considered how you will communicate effectively with professional colleagues whose experiences, beliefs, and assumptions may be different from your own?

Communicate with Cooperating Teacher

Your first few conversations with your cooperating teacher are crucial to your getting off to a good start. They communicate your interest and initiative. They also give you the opportunity to discuss expectations (yours and hers) and to ask questions.

Accordingly, plan your part in those conversations. You may want to brainstorm a few questions to ask your cooperating teacher. In order to for-

Sample Conversation Starters

1. Do you have any suggestions about what I can do to prepare for student teaching with you?
2. What are you looking for in a student teacher? What are your expectations of a student teacher?
3. Where did you complete your student teaching? What was the experience like for you?
4. What can you tell me about the children in your class? Ratio of boys to girls? Minorities? Socioeconomic status? Ability levels?
5. Are there any parent handbooks describing policies such as attendance, illness, guidance, and parental responsibilities that would be helpful for me to read?
6. Are there curriculum guides or written descriptions of developmentally appropriate practices or "best practices" that I will be expected to follow?
7. Are there any written or unwritten policies regarding the day-to-day functioning of the center or school that I should be aware of before I begin student teaching? Is there a dress code for children and for teachers? Are there rules about use of copy machines, use of faculty room, use of telephone?
8. What is the career ladder or hierarchy by which this child development center or school operates? Program director, program manager, principal, etc.?
(Adams, Shea, Liston, & Deever, 1998; Blair & Jones, 1998; McEwan, 2001).

mulate these questions, think about what specific skills you wish to develop or strengthen, what content area thematic units you may wish to develop, what discipline approaches you favor, and what concerns you have regarding children diagnosed with special needs.

In addition to thinking of questions to ask, consider what you want to communicate about yourself to your cooperating teacher. One way of doing this is to imagine yourself in the role of cooperating teacher. What qualities would you want your student teacher to display? Are you looking for a person who demonstrates enthusiasm and excitement? Are you hoping for a student teacher who takes the initiative to jump right in and be an active participant with the children rather than one who remains a passive observer? If you believe you have these characteristics, how are you going to communicate them to your cooperating teacher in those initial conversations? Remember also that your cooperating teacher may be feeling a little nervous about beginning this important mentoring relationship with you, particularly if she has not had many practicum students.

Communicate with Children

You will find that all children, even the youngest ones, are quick to notice the presence of a new face in the room. Your cooperating teacher may suggest an appropriate time for introductions, such as during a morning group time. Notice how children address the adults in your placement; you will want to follow the customary practice when you introduce yourself. Some schools allow children to call teachers by their first name; others prefer a title followed by first name; others require a title followed by last name.

You may want to plan an age-appropriate name game to introduce yourself and to help you learn the children's names. You may want to bring one of your own favorite children's books to share. You might suggest to your cooperating teacher that you create a bulletin board display with pictures and/or objects that reveal interesting information about yourself that you can share with your children. The children will have a natural curiosity about who you are, so expect that they will ask questions of all kinds. Do not be surprised if young children ask personal questions, so think about ways such as humor to deflect questions you do not wish to answer. Remember also that any-

You may want to get off to a good start with your children by preparing an activity to help you learn their names. You may also want to prepare a collage or poster that you can share to introduce yourself to the children.

thing you say about your activities away from school will probably be repeated at home, so use your discretion.

Parents will be curious about who the student teacher is, so you may want to write a brief letter of introduction to send home with each child. Share your letter with your cooperating teacher. She may have some suggestions and/or she may want to add her own personal note to your letter.

Maintain Confidentiality

As you begin your student teaching practicum, you must have heightened sensitivity to the importance of maintaining confidentiality. You will have access to personal family information, school records, and medical information concerning each child in your care. You will observe behaviors that trouble you and others that delight or amuse you.

Remember that some view your role as a teacher to be as sacred as a priest. It is understandable that you may feel uncomfortable with that religious comparison. However, you may find that children and parents confide in you about personal matters. If you find yourself being drawn into conversations that make you feel uncomfortable, then tactfully pass the matter to your cooperating teacher. For example, some parents may view you as an expert in child rearing. They may ask your advice concerning their child's bed-wetting problems or how to prepare their child for the arrival of a new baby. You should direct these parents to your cooperating teacher, who may guide the parents herself or direct them to a supervisor who may, in turn, direct them to professionally trained community resources.

Another aspect of confidentiality relates to professional discretion. Remember not to discuss events using the real name or descriptions of children, parents, or teachers. Keeping your silence is preferable to being considered a gossip. Comments and discussion should be held with your cooperating teacher or your college supervisor in private, not shared with family and friends. Be careful not to discuss specific people or events in the hallway or the teacher's lounge. A comment that is overheard can have extremely detrimental effects.

Communicate with Your Supervisor

If you have been assigned a college supervisor, she will play a vital role in your development. She will be available to offer support not only to you but also to your cooperating teacher. You may wish to talk with her at the beginning of your practicum. A checklist of topics to cover in that initial meeting may be helpful.

Remember that your supervisor can be an invaluable source of information for you, a sounding board with whom you can share your frustrations

---

Sample Topics for Meeting with Supervisor

- Exchange of e-mail addresses, home phone numbers, cell phone numbers
- Requirements such as creation of a student teaching journal, notebook, or dialogue journal
- Frequency of observations
- Format regarding written feedback and discussion related to observations
- Policies regarding illness or personal emergency
- Expectations regarding attendance at professional development workshops, inservice days, or faculty meetings
- Expectations regarding participation in parent conferences or home visits
- Policies regarding student teaching during the college's scheduled holidays
- Procedures regarding final evaluations, recommendations, and certification requirements

---

as well as your joys, your advocate and your supporter. Three-way communication among you, your supervisor, and your cooperating teacher may encourage the sharing of ideas and perspectives.

Communicate with Administration

In your early days at the facility, you may be able to meet the director of the child development center or the building principal. The administrator will be a helpful source of information regarding the history and mission of the school. In addition, she can describe the teaching and learning philosophy that guides educational practice. In many child development centers and schools, the administrator may function as a hands-on learning leader rather than as an inaccessible paper pusher.

The administrator provides the support necessary to ensure that children achieve the intended outcomes (Dufour, 2002). In fact, preservice teachers often declare that "it is the school, not the university [or college], that is the real center of [their] teacher education" (Eisner, 2002, p. 577). Therefore, keep in mind that the administrator, as the school leader, can also add a new dimension to your teacher education.

Communicate with Support Staff

Similarly, you must make yourself known to the support staff as well. The **paraprofessionals**, the secretarial personnel, the custodial staff, and others can make your teaching experience even more pleasant. They play a vital

Paraprofessionals provide direct assistance to children and families; they are supervised by teachers or other trained professionals (Pickett, 1999).

Getting to know your administrator is an important way to get your student teaching off to a good start. Make sure to have a friendly smile and a greeting whenever you see her.

role in the day-to-day operations of the facility. When you need to know the most efficient process for accomplishing routine tasks, the support staff will provide that assistance.

Communicate with Friends and Family

One important area frequently overlooked by students is communication with family and friends, particularly in the early days of the student teaching practicum. Communication is crucial to having a positive experience whether you are a nontraditional age student or a more typical age student commuting or living on campus. In addition, you may be dependent on the income from a job to meet living expenses while you are attending college. These and other personal topics need to be considered.

Whether you are a college student of typical age living on campus or a nontraditional student with multiple off-campus responsibilities, you may want to consider discussing some ground rules to help you and those with whom you live. For example, you may find that you need to develop new routines regarding bed times, early morning preparations for the day, and

Questions Concerning Expectations

- Who are the people I will come in contact with regularly outside of my teaching hours? (family, friends, employers, etc.)
- What demands do I expect these people to make on my time and energy during my practicum?
- How much time and energy do I believe I will be able to give to these people during my practicum?
- What difficulties, if any, can I anticipate? How can I prevent potential difficulties?
- What support system is in place to help me if I have questions or need to brainstorm ideas related to student teaching?
- Does my college have any policies concerning my employment or participation in extracurricular activities while I am completing my practicum?
- Do I have adequate transportation? Do I have a back-up plan in case of transportation difficulties?

social activities. Your changes in behavior may affect other people in your life, so you need to communicate your anticipated needs and expectations if you have not already done so. Some preservice teachers express surprise at the fact that their nonteacher friends and family members have little understanding of how much mental and physical energy they direct toward teaching even when the work day is over.

Unless you are used to working in an early childhood setting, you may find that you must adjust your daily schedule. Some preschool programs require your attendance before 7:00 A.M. because working parents have to drop their children off quite early. Many primary school programs expect teachers to be on duty well before 8:30 A.M. You should get used to arriving no later than your cooperating teacher. In fact, many successful student teachers make a point of arriving well before their cooperating teachers in order to open up the room and have everything ready for the day to begin.

❖ PERSONAL PREPARATIONS

Generally speaking, your college or university will be carefully monitoring the legal and health paperwork necessary for you to participate in your early childhood practicum. You may want to double check just to assure yourself that all necessary forms are in order. Some private locations have additional requirements. Finding this out early can save you unnecessary last-minute stress.

Legal Considerations

Your college or university will be keeping a file containing copies of your criminal background clearance, child abuse clearance, and tuberculin (TB) clearance. Regulations vary from state to state. Public schools and private early childhood centers may also have different requirements. For example, some facilities require that all clearances be current, within the last twelve months. Others accept clearances no older than three months prior to contact with children. Check to see what the regulations are for the facility in which you are preparing to student teach (Machado & Botnarescue, 2001).

Health Considerations

You would be wise to take care of all personal health concerns prior to beginning your student teaching. For example, if you have been putting off an eye exam or a health exam for a chronic problem, then do it right away. You do not want a recurring problem to become an impediment during this important semester.

Some early childhood centers may even require a physician's report assessing your general health. You may not have had a complete physical since enrolling in college. Therefore, a vision and health screening and an assessment of your need for immunizations such as vaccines against influenza or hepatitis B may be beneficial.

In addition, you may be asked for a physician's assessment of your orthopedic, psychological, and neurological functioning. In other words, is there any impediment that may interfere with your ability to work effectively with young children? After all, you may be expected to lift children and supplies, sit on the floor or on small-sized furniture, and move quickly to supervise young children.

Stress Management

Even before you get into the daily momentum of student teaching, you may want to consider a plan for managing stress. Your anxiety level will decrease if you follow the suggestions of effective communication previously discussed. Recognize that some stress can be a positive, energizing response to a new situation. Your attitude is the key to managing stress. Yes, you may occasionally have some anxiety. Yes, you may occasionally feel overwhelmed with responsibilities for planning and teaching. This is normal. You can manage your stress by breaking large tasks into small segments, by thorough lesson preparation, and by positive self-talk.

In any case, the key is how you respond to stress. It may seem obvious; but try to find a way to relax each day, even for ten minutes. Some students

Stress-Related Questions

1. Am I getting daily exercise, even for 10 or 15 minutes?
2. Am I getting enough sleep?
3. Am I getting regular meals?
4. Do I engage in a brief relaxing mental activity unrelated to school, such as a crossword puzzle or easy reading?
5. Am I able to maintain my sense of humor?
6. Do I strive for excellence, not perfection?
7. Do I communicate with other student teachers to discover what works for them?
8. Would I consider counseling if necessary?
   (Machado & Botnarescue, 2001; Roe & Ross 2002)

write in their personal journals daily; others exercise; others meditate. You will find what works for you.

❖ DEVELOPMENT OF A SUPPORT SYSTEM

A certain ambiguity is inherent in all teaching. There is no defined prescription to ensure feelings of calm and confidence. Therefore, the development of a support system is crucial to a successful experience.

Need for a Support System

As a preservice teacher, you find yourself split between two quite different worlds. For eight or more hours per day, you function in the role of teacher, surrounded by professional colleagues. You must meet performance-based standards that describe what teachers must know and do. At the same time, you are expected to enjoy yourself so that your enthusiasm for teaching helps foster a love of learning within each child. These are the daily challenges of the professional community you are joining.

Then, each evening, you return to your other life surrounded by friends and/or family. This split existence can be somewhat unsettling. There will be times you are bursting with excitement to share a highlight from your day. You may find that your nonteaching friends and/or family do not share your same enthusiasm for the stories of your successes in the classroom. Similarly, they may not empathize with your anxieties and self-doubts as you confront new challenges. A sense of isolation can become overwhelming. That is why it is important to create a support system of one or more peers who are sharing similar experiences. Lack of time and exhaustion are common complaints during student teaching. Nevertheless, you may find that phone calls, short dinner breaks, or exercise breaks with fellow student teachers are invaluable opportunities to share experiences and feelings.

Creating a Peer Group Support System

Educators who are dedicated to the concepts of lifelong learning and mutual self-improvement often express a need to talk with colleagues about matters of professional practice. The formation of teacher study groups is one way to create opportunities for dialogue within a community of educators. Birchak and colleagues (1998) promote the formation of voluntary study groups as one way for teachers to eliminate a sense of isolation and competitiveness and to create instead "an investigative environment that supports individually directed growth and influences the school community at large" (p. 143). This concept of study groups may be adapted to meet your needs as an early childhood student teacher.

Accordingly, you and your fellow student teachers may benefit from the formation of supportive groups in order to maintain a sense of community. Students in a group should have a common interest and focus; for example, the early childhood student teaching experience. As with the teacher study groups described by Birchak and colleagues, participation by student teachers should be voluntary. It is important to define the support group by what it is not. It is not a required course; it is neither a workshop nor a seminar. It is a voluntary group of students who are sharing a common experience. They make the group into whatever they want it to be.

Accordingly, the important issue here is that students have a regular opportunity to share important events in their daily lives. They quickly learn that they are not the only ones who sometimes feel fearful, foolish, or frustrated. They share resources and suggestions. At the same time, they take pleasure in each other's accomplishments, whether it is the excitement of helping a child learn a new skill or the pride of receiving a compliment from a cooperating teacher.

As an illustration, one support group of six early childhood student teachers chose to meet every two to three weeks. The general consensus was that although time was severely limited, everyone would take a dinner break at some point. They might as well take that break together. These six students were student teaching at six different schools or child development centers, so they did not come in contact with each other on a regular basis. One student was placed in a large inner-city charter school. One student was in a small urban setting. Four students were placed in suburban settings. They had different supervisors and were teaching children of different ages. The only commonality was that they were all experiencing early childhood student teaching.

In addition, this particular group held its meetings with an education professor who was a participant/observer. Nevertheless, the success of the group was not dependent on the presence of an authority figure or a mentor. The students guided the meetings while the professor took a nondirective role. Comments and reactions from members of this student support group will be interspersed throughout sections of this text as appropriate.

Process of Group Support

Each support group gathering began with a brief time for informal conversations and sharing of recent experiences. Conversations were lively and interspersed with comments like, "That happened to me too; let me tell you about . . . ." Next, students raised questions or concerns for discussion. The group tried to focus the discussion for each session. Topics varied greatly depending on the needs of the group. Some concerns included how to improve communication with the cooperating teacher and how to meet the needs of *all* children. A timekeeper was appointed at each meeting so that the gatherings could be limited to one hour. About ten minutes before time was up, students set a date for the next get-together and agreed on a tentative focus for future discussion.

Benefits of the Support Group

For many of the students, sharing was the primary reason for attending. Hearing about each other's experiences reduced the stress and sense of isolation that can build up during a lengthy student teaching practicum. For others, the focused discussion was the heart of the meeting. The quality of information discussed determined whether students felt their time was spent productively. All students reported that they enjoyed the meetings. Some commented on the developing sense of trust among group members. This trust allowed collaboration to become the group's strength; it created a pathway for mutual improvement during the journey of student teaching.

An added benefit was that students experienced the social nature of learning. They created a community in which communication flowed freely. They made sense of their experiences personally and collectively in a safe environment of their own choosing (Wink & Putney, 2002). In other words, they were experiencing the Vygotskian principles of scaffolding and social interaction they had been taught in their child development classes and in their methods classes. An unintended benefit, therefore, was the personalization of this pedagogical process.

Keeping a Human Connection

You may find that a peer support group is neither possible nor desirable for you because of your particular personal commitments and responsibilities. You may not need such a group because your college already has a class or a required seminar that serves this purpose. If this is not the case in your situation, you may be able to maintain a connection with others by e-mail or by phone. However you do it, the human connection and sense of community will help you maintain your positive outlook as you discover the joys and challenges of teaching.

❖ FINAL THOUGHTS

You have completed all your preparation. You have already made a good first impression by developing your knowledge base about the child development center or school and its demographics. You are communicating with your cooperating teacher. You have discussed your needs and expectations with family and friends. You even have a peer support system available. You feel ready and excited as you begin the early days of your early childhood practicum.

Even so, you may relate to the thoughts of another student teacher written a few hours before dawn of the first day.

Voices of Reality: Student Teacher Speaks

The reality is beginning to hit me. Wow. To say that my feelings are completely jumbled and scrambled and topsy-turvy would be an understatement. On the one hand, I am bubbling with excitement. Fourteen weeks in which to enter the young lives of 20-plus precious individuals and to welcome these children into my own life. The possibilities for touching and helping to shape these lives are endless, and to think that I may have a hand in this impact fills me with warmth from head to toe. On the other hand, I know the awesome responsibility that this entails fills me with more than a little bit of anxiety. Okay, I'll admit it, I'm really, really scared. I wonder if it's normal to feel this unprepared. Classes in teaching and the handful of lessons developed and carried out during Junior Block are one thing, but student teaching . . . that feels like an entirely different ball game—like jumping from the dugout, with an occasional inning of play here and there, to a regular spot in the starting line-up. WOW. Am I up to this challenge? Do I truly have what it takes to be one of those special people who "CAN"? When these questions cause me to doubt my own competency, I reassure myself with the reminder that I already possess two of the most essential tools of an educator: an intense love of children, and a great desire to become a lasting influence upon young minds and hearts.

Karla S.

ACTIVITIES FOR REFLECTION AND ACTION

1. List the questions and/or concerns you have about starting your teaching experience. Then identify one or more resources you can use to answer each of your questions and to ease your concerns.

2. Does your practicum site have the following personnel?

Position	Yes	No	Name(s)	Location
Director/Principal				
Clerical Staff				
Maintenance Staff				
Health Services				
Paraprofessionals				
Special Needs Support Staff				
Community Liaison Staff				
Others				

3. What do you know about cultural character of the children at your practicum site? For each cultural group represented, find the answers to the following questions (Fuller, 2001):
   - What are the famous names and events that have shaped the history of each cultural group?
   - Who are the famous people in each cultural group who may serve as positive role models?
   - What are the major religious and political beliefs of each cultural group?
   - What are the celebration days of each cultural group?
   - What is the native language of each cultural group?
   - What are the current economic, political, and social issues that concern each cultural group?

4. How will you collect the information you need on the cultural groups represented among your children? Make a list of potential sources of information. Be specific with regard to print or technology resources. Consider places to visit such as community agencies and cultural organizations.

To analyze some mini-cases and take some practice quizzes related to the content of this chapter, log on to the Companion Website at www.prenhall.com/tyminski. Go to Chapter 1 and choose from the links in the left column.

CHAPTER 2

Becoming a Professional

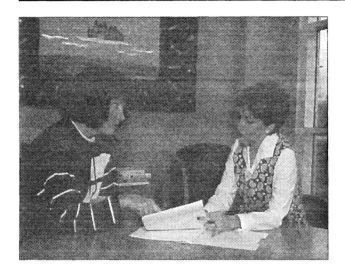

Teaching is a process of becoming that continues throughout life, never completely achieved, never completely denied. This is the challenge and the fun of being a teacher—there is no ultimate end to the process.

Frances Mayforth

As a student teacher, you are already considered to be a professional. Nevertheless, you are in the initial stages of what will become a lifelong journey of learning more about yourself, about the children in your care, and about the facilitation of the teaching-learning process. You have probably heard the expression, "The more you learn, the more you realize you do not know." This is particularly true in early childhood education. We are only beginning to appreciate the impact of research on the brain development of infants and young children. For example, studies indicate that a baby is born with only 25% of its brain developed; but by age three, 90% of its brain is developed (Benesh, Arbuckle, Robbins, & D'Arcangelo, 1998; Governor's Commission, 2000; D'Arcangelo, 2000; Wolfe & Brandt, 1998). So, as an early childhood educator, you have important opportunities to provide the healthy, stimulating, caring environment children need for a lifetime of success. What an amazing opportunity to shape the future!

Initially, you may have been drawn to the profession of teaching because you want to make a difference in children's lives. Perhaps you will remain in this profession because you enjoy the never-ending fun and challenge of learning along with your children. The simultaneous frustration and joy of teaching young children is that you can indeed make a difference in children's lives; but you may not know for a long time, if ever, the full impact of your influence. Your journey down the road of lifelong learning and professional development is truly one that can never be fully achieved or fully denied.

During the early weeks of your student teaching, perhaps you are experiencing some of the feelings expressed by these students concerning becoming a teaching professional.

As already stated, you are viewed as a professional from the moment you step into a childcare facility or a school-based early childhood classroom. Accordingly, the expectation is that you conduct yourself with "professionalism." The term requires some explanation.

❖ WHAT IT MEANS TO BE A PROFESSIONAL

Consideration of what it means to be a professional is extremely important in early childhood education just as in any other area of teaching. However, you will be called on not only to teach but also to advocate for the youngest, most vulnerable, and most powerless of all humanity. Therefore, you must be acutely aware of professional standards of practice when making decisions.

Terminology

As recently as the 1990s, some early childhood educators voiced discomfort with the use of the word *professional* as a noun to refer to early childhood teachers. To them, it implied a sense of separation or elitism. Although they

---

Voices of Reality: Student Teachers Speak

This morning I had the opportunity to lead the class. . . . The students' responses provided ideal springboards for discussions. I absolutely love these moments when I feel so completely "teacher-y!"

Karla S.

One of the boys in my morning class said, "Why does Mrs. K. have to go to school, I thought she already knows everything." I told them that you can always learn something new everyday. That had another student say, "Just like you, huh, Miss F.?" And I believe that is true 100%, you do learn something at any point in time on any day, at any age. "Real" teachers are always learning too.

Nancy F.

As I move closer and closer to "professional" status as a teacher, I have found myself viewing a professional as highly dynamic. Being a professional means always striving to be better.

Saul D.

called for high standards of practice, they associated the term *professional* with persons whose work is specialized and selective (Bredekamp & Willer, 1993; Fromberg, 1997). Others, the author included, do not believe that specialization and selectivity are necessarily bad things. Think about how you define the word *professional.* Does a particular image come to mind? Is this image in tune with your image of yourself as an early childhood teacher?

In contrast, the word *professional* used as an adjective created positive responses in the past as well as now. No one can argue with the implication that early childhood educators should exhibit ethical conduct and be knowledgeable individuals (Bredekamp & Willer, 1993). *Professionalism* is behavior characterized by common descriptors (Beaty, 2004; Fromberg, 1997; NAEYC [National Association for the Education of Young Children], 2001b; Whitehead, 1929):

1. Adherence to an ethical code of conduct
2. Demonstrated sense of commitment and service to others
3. Demonstrated mastery of a specialized body of knowledge
4. Demonstrated ability to consciously *use* the specialized knowledge acquired
5. Attainment of established standards and practices that control entry into the profession
6. Membership in a professional organization that affects professional policy and activity
7. Commitment to ongoing professional development

You may wish to add your own ideas to this list of descriptors as you reflect on what *becoming a professional* means to you.

Ethical Guidelines and Professional Standards

According to Bredekamp and Willer (1993), a defining characteristic of a profession is a shared code of ethics. As an early childhood professional, you have a code of ethics to guide your own behavior and to monitor the behavior of others. At some point during your early childhood courses, you may have read and discussed the NAEYC Code of Ethical Conduct. If not, this is an appropriate time to do so. Even if you have reviewed it in the past, this would be a good time to take another look at the Code in Figure 2.1. Certain shared values are inherent in these standards of ethical behavior. One important aspect of becoming a professional is committing yourself to these values. Therefore, as you begin student teaching, you may want to reaffirm your personal commitment suggested in the NAEYC Code of Ethical Conduct (Figure 2.2).

This affirmation of professional ideals is a good beginning. Your knowledge of the Code and your commitment to its values are merely the starting

Ethical Responsibilities to Children

P-1.1 Above all, we shall not harm children in any way. We shall not participate in practices that are disrespectful, degrading, dangerous, exploitative, intimidating, psychologically damaging, or physically harmful to children. This principle has precedence over all others in this Code.

P-1.2 We shall not participate in any practices that discriminate against children by denying benefits, giving special advantages, or excluding them from programs or activities on the basis of their race, religion, gender, national origin, language, ability, or the status, behavior, or beliefs of their parents. (This principle does not apply to programs that have a lawful mandate to provide services to a particular population of children.)

P-1.3 We shall involve all those with relevant knowledge (including staff and parents) in decisions concerning a child.

P-1.5 We shall be familiar with the symptoms of child abuse, including physical, sexual, verbal, and emotional abuse, and neglect.

P-1.6 When we have reasonable cause to suspect child abuse or neglect, we shall report it to the appropriate community agency and follow up to ensure that appropriate action has been taken. When appropriate, parents or guardians will be informed that the referral has been made.

FIGURE 2.1 Abbreviated Overview of Code of Ethical Conduct

To the best of my ability I will

- Ensure that programs for young children are based on current knowledge of child development and early childhood education.
- Respect and support families in their task of nurturing children.
- Respect colleagues in early childhood education and support them in maintaining the NAEYC Code of Ethical Conduct.
- Serve as an advocate for children, their families, and their teachers in community and society.
- Maintain high standards of professional conduct.
- Recognize how personal values, opinions, and biases can affect professional judgment.
- Be open to new ideas and be willing to learn from the suggestions of others.
- Continue to learn, grow, and contribute as a professional.
- Honor the ideals and principles of the NAEYC Code of Ethical Conduct.

FIGURE 2.2 Statement of Commitment

Your cooperating teacher and your college supervisor can provide helpful guidance when you are unsure how to handle a situation to which there is no clear answer. Their perspectives are based on years of experience as well as education.

points. You must use these guidelines as the foundation on which you make ethical judgments. As you proceed through your student teaching experience, situations will arise in which your decisions will have consequences for children, families, and perhaps the community. You may have more than one ethical response to problem-solving situations. One source of help is the NAEYC Code of Ethical Conduct. Other sources of help include your cooperating teacher and your college supervisor. Although the Code does not contain solutions to specific situations, it is a reference point for decision making that was developed by a consensus of professionals in your field (Brophy-Herb, Kostelnik, & Stein, 2001).

The Code of Ethical Conduct and Ethical Dilemmas

You may find that dilemmas requiring ethical judgments occur early during your student practicum. For example, in the second week of the semester, Angie D., a student teacher, reports a situation that makes her uncomfortable. A child in first grade who is diagnosed with mental retardation is pulled out of the room to receive learning support in math each day. When he returns, the other children are just beginning their math lesson. Current practice has been to occupy the child with a paper to color or to give him the same math worksheet as the more typical students. When he becomes disruptive (which is a daily occurrence), he is removed from class "for the greater good of the remaining students." The student teacher feels bad for the little boy, but she does not want to "rock the boat" with her cooperating teacher. Her peers empathize and suggest the following problem-solving options:

- Ask your college supervisor for advice.
- Talk with your cooperating teacher and brainstorm other ways to handle the situation, such as rescheduling math time, adapted activities for the child, and so on.
- Perhaps your cooperating teacher can ask for a team meeting with the special education teacher, parent, and so on to brainstorm and develop alternatives.
- Above all, think of the child first and do *something!*

No one in the student teacher support group mentioned the Code of Ethical Conduct. Nevertheless, that is perhaps the most important starting point when deciding what to do or say in a difficult situation involving young children. It may help you discover the insights of other professionals. It may help you find the personal courage to make ethical decisions that reflect best practices for *all* children (Feeney, Christensen, & Moravcik, 2001; Freeman, 2000). According to Freeman (2000), the NAEYC Code of Ethics "is specific enough to guide those who need strength to shoulder their ethical responsibilities and those struggling to resolve thorny dilemmas" (p. 14).

In the case mentioned by Angie D., the Code of Ethical Conduct is helpful. Section p-1.2 reminds us that we should not exclude children from programs or activities for reasons such as difference in ability. Section p-1.3 reminds us that we should involve others, including parents, in the planning process in order to meet each child's needs. These sections and others helped guide Angie D. as she addressed her concerns with her cooperating teacher. In this case, the general education teacher, the student teacher, the special education teacher, and the parents met to brainstorm solutions. As a result, math schedules were modified by the general education teacher, and math activities were adapted by the special education teacher so this child could be included more effectively with his peers.

Confidentiality

Angie D.'s discussion of her concerns brings to mind another aspect of becoming a professional, the importance of confidentiality. Even if you disagree with your cooperating teacher, another colleague, or a parent, you must not vent your feelings or opinions to others in the faculty room, the hallways, or outside the facility. If you need to discuss confidential matters that occur in your classroom, wait until you can schedule uninterrupted time with your cooperating teacher or wait until you can visit with your college supervisor. In the case of the student support group mentioned above, Angie D. was careful not to mention particular names; and students were able to voice concerns with the knowledge that the matters discussed "would not leave that room."

Written Sources for Professional Decision Making

Although you may not be faced with the same dilemma as Angie D., you will encounter other problems for which you do not have an immediate solution. Therefore, during your student teaching practicum, you may want to start a notebook of relevant guidelines and regulations to help you make professional decisions. A copy of the NAEYC Code of Ethical Conduct should certainly be included. You may also locate written policies regarding the reporting of suspected child abuse, school attendance, rights of children with disabilities and their parents, childcare licensing regulations, and educational standards at the national, state, and local level. You may also find it useful to include NAEYC's Position Statements on a variety of topics. These may be obtained from NAEYC's Web site *www.naeyc.org*. You will feel more comfortable making ethical judgments and discussing best practices for *All* young children when you have easy access to such information.

Knowledge and Critical Reflection

Another aspect of becoming a professional is demonstrated ability to make decisions grounded in sound theory and practice. You must be knowledgeable about current research findings and reflect on the implications of these findings. As you dialogue with professional colleagues in the workplace and at conferences, you will discover multiple perspectives concerning what constitutes *best practice*. You may want to collect a file of ideas on such topics as suggestions for organizing newsletters, recommendations for conducting class meetings, and research-based findings about conflict resolution and peer mediation strategies. Helpful Web sites and locations and phone numbers of community agencies would also be appropriate to keep on file.

As your collection of information and current research grows, you may find that you have multiple perspectives that differ in their approach to central questions. Therefore, you will have to become a critical, reflective practitioner as you make decisions based on the context of your particular early childhood community. Your cooperating teacher and your college supervisor

---

Sample Web Sites for Resources File

- **American Federation of Teachers Educational Foundation (AFTEF)** with which the Center for Childcare Workforce merged in 2002. Now includes a focus on early childhood pre-K issues such as staffing needs and qualifications.
  www.aft.org
- **Council for Exceptional Children (CEC)** Web site provides up-to-date information on all aspects of the education and development of students who have disabilities or students who are considered gifted.
  www.cec.sped.org
- **Early Head Start National Resource Center @ ZERO TO THREE** with links to resources and information focusing on the first three years of life.
  www.ehsnrc.org
- **Federal Interagency Coordinating Council** focuses on children ages zero to eight who may be considered "at risk" and their families with links to resources and current research. Information in Spanish and English.
  www.fed-icc.org/
- **Frank Porter Graham Child Development Center** at the University of North Carolina at Chapel Hill provides research and educational information with focus on child development and health.
  www.fpg.unc.edu
- **National Association for Family Child Care (NAFCC)** Web site focuses on improvement of family and group child care with information and assistance for providers.
  www.nafcc.org
- **NAEYC** Web site for information on readiness indicators, standards, best practices, and professional development opportunities.
  www.naeyc.org/childrens_champions/issues.asp
- **National Child Care Information Center** Web site provides a national clearinghouse, technical assistance, and linkages to information about early child care and education. Links include faith-based initiatives, fatherhood, rural families, welfare reform, and many other priorities.
  www.nccic.org

---

will be helpful resources as you assimilate these perspectives and formulate your own reflective approach to teaching.

Identification and Involvement

An important step in becoming a professional is to involve yourself with others who share your interest in the early childhood field. You need to become identified with colleagues who understand what being a professional means. One of the best ways to do this is to join a professional organization such as NAEYC. Students generally have limited financial resources, but student memberships are available at a reduced rate. It is not too late to join at the student rate if you have not already done so.

This connection with your professional organization identifies you with over 100,000 teachers, administrators, parents, and others who share your commitment to high-quality education and care of young children. The benefits for students outweigh the costs. For example, membership entitles you to receive a journal containing the most recent developments in your field and access to a members-only Web site at no extra charge. Other opportunities, such as attendance at conferences and seminars, are available at a reduced fee. Perhaps the most important benefit of student memberships is the heightened awareness that you share a knowledge base and a history with respected professionals worldwide.

This is but a small sample of the organizations available to offer information, advocacy, and support for you as an early childhood teacher as well as for the parents and community agencies with whom you come in contact. You can check out the professional development opportunities by going online or by writing these organizations and others with similar goals. You may

---

Examples of Professional Organizations

American Montessori Society (AMS)
150 Fifth Avenue
New York, NY 10011
(journal: *Montessori Life*)

Association for Childhood Education International (ACEI)
7904 Georgia Avenue, Suite 215
Olney, MD 20832
(journal: *Childhood Education*)

Council for Exceptional Children (CEC)
1110 North Glebe Road, Suite 300
Arlington, VA 22201-5704
(journal: *Teaching Exceptional Children*)

National Association for Bilingual Education (NABE)
1030 15th St., NW, Suite 470
Washington, DC 20005-1503
(journal: *Bilingual Research Journal*)

National Association for the Education of Young Children (NAEYC)
1509 16th St., NW
Washington, DC 2006-1426
(journal: *Young Children*)

Child Welfare League of America (CWLA)
440 First Street, NW, Third Floor
Washington, DC 20001-2085

Ecumenical Child Care Network
P.O. Box 803536
Chicago, IL 60680

soon find that your work with diverse young children and their families will lead you in many diverse directions of professional development.

Professionalism and Lifelong Learning

Another aspect of becoming a professional is the recognition that you are embarking on a process of lifelong learning. Your student teaching practicum is an important milestone in your career development, but it is only the beginning of your professional growth. Presumably, throughout your education courses, you have engaged in collaborative learning with other students, your professors, and the cooperating teachers from previous field experiences. This exchange of ideas with colleagues will continue to be an integral part of your professional development.

Throughout your student teaching practicum, avail yourself of all opportunities to learn from colleagues. Attend inservice training experiences. If possible, accompany your cooperating teacher to educational workshops and/or conferences.

Equally important, form connections with professionals from disciplines related to early childhood education. This may sound like unusual advice at a time when you may be just getting to know your cooperating teacher, the children, and their families. Nevertheless, you need to know the specialists who serve your diverse population of children. If you understand the roles of these other professionals, you will know when and how to access the skills and expertise they offer. Therefore, ask your cooperating teacher for assistance in meeting the special educators, the reading specialist, the school psychologist, the English as a second language specialist, the speech and language therapist, and others. Since many children who have special needs of one kind or another are now included in early childhood programs with their typical peers, your collaboration with colleagues of other disciplines is more critical than ever before.

Professional Growth as a Team Member

During your student teaching practicum, seek opportunities to observe and/or participate in any transdisciplinary team meetings that are held. These are meetings attended by people across *(trans)* various disciplines who come together with the child's parents or guardians to coordinate services and develop plans for improving a child's functioning. One significant characteristic of transdisciplinary teams is that people share information and learn from each other; services are coordinated with each other rather than performed in isolation.

Therefore, you may be sitting around a table with the child's parents, your cooperating teacher, a communication disorder specialist, a nurse, an ad-

Participating as a team member is one of the most important experiences you can have as a student teacher. You will observe educators and parents learn from each other, solve problems, and make decisions as a team.

ministrator, a psychologist, a behavior specialist, and other support staff. Such teaming may occur for the purpose of developing an Individual Family Service Plan (IFSP) for a child below the age of three or an Individual Education Plan (IEP) for a child beginning at age three who has special needs. A transdisciplinary team meeting may also be held to discuss observations or formal assessment results of a child who seems to be developing in an atypical manner.

If you have a chance to participate in a transdisciplinary team meeting, you will see how team members share information, resolve conflicts of opinion, generate creative ideas to find solutions, and collaborate to make decisions. You may even be called on to share your observations. You will see for yourself how effective communication skills can lead to positive relationships between parents and professionals. You may also take some comfort in the knowledge that "no one person assumes more responsibility than another; all are held accountable together" (Westling & Fox, 2000, p. 52). In addition, you may learn helpful information that you can take back and implement right away. An effective team approach is therefore beneficial to all participants. It can be an opportunity for learning and professional growth.

Becoming a Professional Member of the Workplace

Your overall appearance, including your clothing, your grooming, and your demeanor, contributes to your image as a member of the professional workplace. Some schools or child development programs have written dress codes. Others do not. If you are not sure how to dress, then choose conservative clothing.

Although most student teachers dress appropriately in the workplace, once in a while, students make inappropriate choices. These unfortunate choices may result in embarrassment for the student and for the person who finds it necessary to discuss the matter with the student. This difficulty can be easily avoided by following a few guidelines.

You may be able to add to these suggestions or alter them as you talk with your cooperating teacher or college supervisor.

In addition, you should be aware of your grooming and your demeanor. Hairstyles, for example, should, like clothing, be conservative. A smile on your face even if you do not feel well sends a positive message to others. These personal areas of dress, grooming, and demeanor can go a long way toward helping you become an accepted member of the professional community.

In the early days of your field experience or student teaching, you are told about attendance policies. Make sure that you remain vigilant about your punctuality and attendance. Professional teachers usually prefer to work even when they are not feeling well. They frequently arrive early and stay

---

Typical Guidelines for Professional Dress

- Make sure that when you bend over, your shirt or sweater does not rise up to expose bare skin.
- Make sure that if you wear white or light-colored clothing, no undergarments show through the fabric.
- Generally avoid perfumes, colognes, or aftershaves. They may be distracting or cause allergic reactions.
- Generally remove nose rings, eyebrow rings, lip or tongue rings, or any other piercings that may be a distraction.
- Women should observe the accepted practice regarding hemlines on skirts or dresses at the field experience site. As a general rule, longer is better.
- Some schools have a policy prohibiting sneakers, sandals, and flip flops. Check with your cooperating teacher to find out the policy at your location.
- Avoid clothing or jewelry that makes a political or religious statement. For example, some schools will not allow religious jewelry to be worn by either children or adults.

late. You may find that you do likewise as you progress through the weeks of your student teaching experience.

Becoming an Informed Professional

One final element of becoming a professional involves keeping abreast of current issues and the policy-making process. As a student teacher, you should be cognizant of societal concerns regarding the quality of early childhood programs. These concerns will affect you in areas such as financial compensation, assessment, and standards. Therefore, it is in your best interest to know who makes these decisions and how these policies are implemented.

One way of keeping informed is to maintain your connection with your early childhood professional organization, NAEYC. Periodically, check their links regarding advocacy and recent developments. For example, the NAEYC home page maintains a site called Children's Champions through which you can access an Action Center. This Action Center allows you to e-mail your state's members of Congress regarding critical issues impacting early childhood education. Through this link, you may also discover federal and state policies and legislation that affect young children. As a student teacher, your time is severely limited; but you may find it worthwhile to be aware of issues that impact your life in such a direct manner. In addition, your advocacy can make a difference in the lives of young children who have no voice in these matters.

❖ PROFESSIONAL ISSUES RELATED TO EARLY CHILDHOOD

You are entering the field of early childhood education at an exciting time of change. You have an obligation to yourself, to your colleagues, and to your children to be acutely aware of trends and current issues affecting your field. Your future depends on your awareness and your professional involvement.

Public Perception

Early childhood education has been called "a public relations nightmare" (Fromberg, 1997, p. 188). A common misperception is that anyone who is nurturing and motherly can use common sense to care for infants and young children. So-called dual systems of early childhood care through public schools and nonpublic settings may have contributed to this viewpoint (Fromberg, 1997).

Thankfully, the status of early childhood care is gradually changing as nonpublic settings are becoming accredited. For example, many families choose family childcare for their young children. More and more of these home providers are becoming so-called master providers who are regulated by organizations such as the National Association for Family Child Care (NAFCC). NAFCC accreditation is a voluntary commitment to professionalism that at least 1,500 family childcare providers undertook in 2001 (Eaton, 2002). These providers consider themselves to be lifelong learners who are committed to providing high-quality childcare (Weaver, 2002). They still represent a minority of providers, however. Therefore, your challenge will be to be an advocate for your profession as you interact with the public.

Compensation

Another area of concern in pre-K early childhood education is inadequate compensation for qualified teachers. According to the federal Bureau of Labor Statistics, in 1999, the average childcare worker earned an average of $15,430; and preschool teachers earned an average of $19,610. These figures represent less than half of what the average elementary school teacher earned during the same period. In fact, "as a nation, the United States pays about as much to parking-lot attendants and dry-cleaning workers as it does to early-childhood educators" (Executive Summary, 2002, p. 9). No wonder the profession is plagued by high turnover rates of personnel!

The United States government's support of childcare in this country is ranked among the lowest in the civilized world (NAEYC, 2001a). Now, before you despair and consider changing your career choice, you should know that there are some positive examples of financing childcare. For example, in the 1980s, the military implemented an affordable, high quality, well-financed childcare system funded by Congress. In the 1990s, North Carolina implemented the Teacher Education and Compensation Helps (T.E.A.C.H.) Project to provide funding for education of employees in regulated childcare programs. The T.E.A.C.H. Model, linking scholarship to increased compensation, has now been implemented in at least twenty-two states (Executive Summary, 2002).

As a professional beginning your career, what can you do? NAEYC suggests the following:

- Read position papers and join the NAEYC interest forum on financing so you will be knowledgeable enough to engage in discussions of early child care financing options.
- Attend professional conferences and attend sessions on finance.
- Join with others in your state to call for a well-financed system of early childhood care.
- Join with other organizations that call for a national dialogue on what is needed to adequately finance childcare.

In other words, consider becoming an advocate for your profession.

Increased Demand for Early Education

The good news is that early childhood education is receiving more and more attention as research continues to document its benefits (Barnett, 2002; Barnett & Camilli, 2002; Olson, 2002). In fact, "Senator Zell Miller, the former governor of Georgia, has called preschool 'the most important grade'" (Barnett & Hustedt, 2003, p. 57). His sentiments are echoed by others across the country.

In fact, Georgia mandates statewide universal pre-K for all four-year-old children, regardless of income. Other states are beginning to follow suit, including New York, Oklahoma, and Florida. The United States has a long way to go on this issue, but at least progress is being made. You, as a new professional, have an opportunity to be an important part of this change in the public's perception of early childhood education.

Shortage of Early Childhood Teachers

According to the U.S. Department of Education (1997), a shortage of early childhood teachers exists nationwide. The turnover rate is approximately 30%, due in part to low wages. The current movement toward universal pre-K classes will only increase the demand for qualified personnel (Whitebook, Sakai, Gerber, & Howes, 2001).

Meeting this demand will take time. In order to become qualified early childhood professionals, people need to complete courses or programs or study, pass standardized testing, and obtain varying amounts of experience. Then they may receive professional credentials. NAEYC lists six different levels of early childhood professionals in Figure 2.3.

Examine these levels and determine where you will be when you complete the program in which you are currently enrolled. These levels also indicate opportunities you may want to consider for future growth as well. They represent one approach to increasing awareness of early childhood education as a profession.

❖ FINAL THOUGHTS

As you can tell, living the life of a professional is a complex mission. Professionalism affects every aspect of your life. You will be holding yourself to high standards of dress, behavior, punctuality, attendance, professional development, and communication with children and their families, colleagues, and members of the community. In many respects, you will be held to a higher standard of expectations than people who work at a job. Many educators, including the author, believe that you are not preparing for a job; you are preparing for a profession. Think about why such a distinction might be made.

Level I

- Working under supervision in an early childhood professional role. Participating in training leading to assessment of competencies or degree.

Level II

- Successful completion of Child Development Associate (CDA) Professional Preparation Program or successful completion of training program leading to CDA Credential through direct assessment.
- Successful completion of one-year early childhood certificate training program.

Level III

- Successful completion of associate degree from NAEYC approved program, or
- Successful completion of associate degree plus 30 units of early childhood development studies or education with 300 hours supervised teaching experience in early childhood, or
- Successful demonstration of meeting outcomes of associate degree program conforming to NAEYC guidelines.

Level IV

- Successful completion of baccalaureate degree from NAEYC approved program, or
- State certification meeting NAEYC or NCATE guidelines, or
- Successful completion of baccalaureate degree in another area with at least 30 units in early childhood development/education including 300 hours of supervised teaching experience, including 150 hours each for at least two of the following age groups: infants and toddlers, 3- to 5-year-olds, or primary grades, or
- Successful demonstration of meeting outcomes of NAEYC approved baccalaureate degree program.

Level V

- Successful completion of master's degree in prescribed program conforming to NAEYC guidelines, or
- Successful demonstration of meeting outcomes of NAEYC approved master's degree program.

Level VI

- Successful completion of a Ph.D. or Ed.D. in prescribed program meeting NAEYC guidelines, or
- Successful demonstration of meeting outcomes of NAEYC approved doctoral degree program.

FIGURE 2.3 Levels of Early Childhood Professionals

Voices of Reality: Student Teachers Speak

When I think of the word "professional" I think of being the best that someone can be. The criteria would be as follows: (1) Act professionally, (2) Dress professionally, (3) Give up some of your college habits . . . hmm . . . , (3) Keep children's names/gossip to yourself even though it might be hard. The list could go on and on. I believe that everyone has their own way of being a professional, but my question is, "Is there a right way or a wrong way to be a professional?"

Jackson L.

Teaching is an interesting profession in that we are not always seen as professional, despite training and knowledge. Being a professional teacher involves so many different facets, including teacher, counselor, nurse, and unfortunately sometimes parent.

Krista U.

A professional manages and balances responsibilities to students, parents, fellow teachers, administrators, and the district at large.

Saul D.

A professional is someone who is involved in a particular line of work for their livelihood.

Nancy F.

As you read the chapters in this text, keep in mind what it means to be a professional and how you can relate your sense of professionalism to every aspect of teaching young children. You may develop your own definition of what it means to be a professional. Perhaps you can relate to the comments made by the student teachers.

ACTIVITIES FOR REFLECTION AND ACTION

1. Create your own definition of what it means to be a professional. Look back at this definition at the end of your student teaching practicum and see if your perspective has changed.
2. Put a copy of the NAEYC Code of Ethical Conduct in your student teaching notebook or journal. Refer to it when in doubt as to the "right" thing to do in a given situation. Keep a record of any dilemmas or "tough decisions" you encounter and how you handled them.

3. Visit a Web site for two or three professional organizations that you might consider joining. List the benefits of each organization. For example, do they offer journals, newsletters, and books to their members? Do they have local, state, and/or national conferences? Do they offer discounts on services of any kinds? What fees are charged for memberships?

 To analyze some mini-cases and take some practice quizzes related to the content of this chapter, log on to the Companion Website at www. prenhall.com/tyminski. Go to Chapter 2 and choose from the links in the left column.

CHAPTER 3

Establishing Effective Professional Relationships

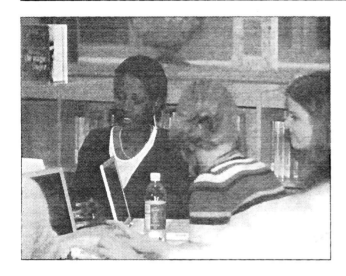

In seeking knowledge, the first step is silence, the second listening, the third remembering, the fourth practicing, and the fifth—teaching others.

Solomon Ibn Gabirol

Solomon lbn Gabirol's words may seem somewhat enigmatic. They contain, however, basic elements necessary for a successful student teaching experience. As you begin the most important field experience of your education so far, you are obviously seeking knowledge that you cannot gain from a textbook alone. Part of your first few days will be spent in watchful silence. You will listen to the sounds of learning as children interact with each other and with the teacher. You will remember your education courses and compare theory to practice. You have the core knowledge necessary to be successful. Now you practice the application of your skills as you begin teaching children and reflecting on the teaching-learning process. You are beginning your lifelong journey along the path of becoming a skillful teacher.

In the early days of your student teaching practicum, you may be wondering how to optimize your relationship with the one person you will be spending most of your waking life with over the next few months—your cooperating teacher.

❖ ESTABLISHING A POSITIVE RELATIONSHIP WITH COOPERATING TEACHERS

The relationship you have with your cooperating teacher is perhaps the single most important factor in determining whether or not you have a successful student teaching experience. It can be a source of joy or extreme

Voices of Reality: Student Teachers Speak

Ah, the first days of school. So many questions and decisions. What should I wear? Will my teacher like me? What should I take? Not only were these questions running through the minds of the students, but also me! Once I calmed myself down, I was ready to walk through the doors of the school as an official student teacher!

First person I saw when I walked in the office was none other than my co-op with a smile on her face. Although I had met her several times before, it was still great to see her bright and early in the morning!

Rosa K.

anxiety (Morris & Morris, 1980). Increasing your awareness of several key issues will help you develop the productive working relationship you desire (Knowles & Cole, 1996).

Differing Types of Cooperating Teachers

You cannot assume that your current cooperating teacher will have the same perspective as teachers in your previous field placements. In fact, you will quickly discover that your cooperating teacher may even have a different outlook on the student teaching process than the teacher down the hall. Sudzina, Giebelhaus, and Coolican (1997) distinguish between two mentoring styles of cooperating teachers. Mentors characterized by Style One may view themselves as older and wiser guides who are in control. With this control style mentor, the student teacher's role is one of being an attentive follower who models the mentor's teaching style. She is expected to accept constructive criticism amiably, work hard, and gradually assume more responsibilities within the classroom. In contrast, Style Two mentors may characterize themselves as supportive partners who share their classrooms, their children, their knowledge, and their responsibilities. This partner style mentor may be attentive to the student teacher's feelings while still expecting cooperation and a willingness to accept criticism. Both parties negotiate and accommodate their needs. The student teacher's role, therefore, is one of being a learner who also has valuable resources to share with the teacher (Machado & Botnarescue, 2001; Sudzina, Giebelhaus, & Coolican, 1997).

Invited Guest/Participant

Although you may encounter other types of cooperating teachers, you must realize the need to be flexible and adapt your behaviors. You are, after all, being invited into your cooperating teacher's classroom with the understanding that you will take every opportunity to learn from that person. You are an invited guest who is expected to be an active participant. Your awareness of this guest/participant status may be particularly crucial if you are placed with a teacher whose philosophy of teaching differs from your own. Accordingly, much of the success of this experience ultimately depends on you.

Establishing a Successful Mentoring Relationship

Think about what kind of relationship you want with your cooperating teacher. Do you want her to be your teacher, your encourager, your role model, your friend, your advisor? With careful thought, attention to some basic communication skills, and planning, you will improve the likelihood of building the kind of relationship you desire.

You may be able to negotiate a regular time to meet and discuss questions and concerns. This planning will also promote the conversation necessary to develop a collaborative mentoring relationship with your cooperating teacher in which the two of you can learn from each other.

Remember that the mentor relationship is not limited to you and your cooperating teacher. Your college supervisor can also be a **mentor** to both of you. She is available to provide support and professional development. This

Mentor refers to a person who serves as a trusted guide, an advisor, a teacher, and an "encourager" of reflective thought (Schon, 1983).

Meetings with your cooperating teacher allow you to discuss events of the day and plan your future activities. This is an opportunity for you to receive feedback and ask for advice.

Sample Topics to Encourage Dialogue

- One of your successes as a student teacher this day/week
- Your greatest concern at this time
- What you are doing to create a warm, caring environment for children
- How you can tell when children are learning
- Insights gained about the art of teaching, in other words, your own "A-HA moments"

(Boreen, Johnson, Niday, & Potts, 2000)

can be a three-way partnership in which all of you benefit from reflective discussions (Boreen, Johnson, Niday, & Potts, 2000).

When you and your mentor begin these reflective discussions, you may find it helpful to have a specific topic on which to focus your dialogue. The following suggestions may give you the starting point needed to commence the conversational flow and exchange of ideas.

Beginning these conversations may not always be easy. Experienced teachers often make decisions intuitively without time for a formal problem-solution process (Bey & Holmes, 1992). Nevertheless, talking about the process of teaching and learning is important. As noted by Richert (1992), when "teachers talk about their work and 'name' their experiences, they learn about what they know and what they believe. They also learn what they do not know. Such knowledge empowers the individual by providing a source for action" (p. 197). Therefore, such dialogue may prove to be mutually beneficial.

❖ ESTABLISHING A POSITIVE RELATIONSHIP WITH YOUR COLLEGE SUPERVISOR

Although many educators believe that your cooperating teacher has more of an impact on your performance than anyone else, your college supervisor is another person who plays an important role in helping you have a successful student teaching experience. Your supervisor will interact with you and your cooperating teacher to define your roles, to set expectations for your performance, and to establish procedures for your evaluation.

When visiting to observe your teaching, she may use techniques to encourage you to analyze your behavior and solve problems yourself. One common practice is to hold a preconference in which you will specify an area in which you would like to have feedback. Then, at the end of the lesson or activity, she may ask you to write down your strengths, your areas of need improvement, and things to do differently next time. In so doing, you will be developing the skills of critical reflection that you will use throughout your professional career (Valli, 1992). This process, called nondirective supervision, may seem frustrating at first because it is much easier to have someone just tell you directly what you are doing well and what you can improve on. Nevertheless, it is a highly effective approach that is commonly practiced (Glickman, 1981). Different supervisors use different techniques. This is something you can discuss during your conferences.

In addition, your supervisor is the liaison between you and your cooperating teacher. If a situation should arise that you do not know how to handle regarding interactions with your cooperating teacher, with children, or with others, call on your college supervisor for assistance. You may also want to invite her to observe special activities in addition to her regularly scheduled visits. The more collegiality there is among you, your cooperating teacher, and your college supervisor, the more comfortable you are likely to feel in your practicum site. Therefore, effective communication skills will be a key ingredient in developing positive relationships.

(**Note:** Observations and assessments of several types will be discussed in more detail in Chapter 6.)

Typical Functions of College Supervisors

- Liaison between school or child development center and college
- Mentor to student teacher
- Mentor to cooperating teacher providing support and professional development
- Hold seminars for student teachers as desired
- Provide immediate feedback to encourage student teacher's professional development
- Hold individual and three-way conferences with student and cooperating teacher to discuss needs and progress
- Write final evaluations and letters of recommendation to school districts and college placement offices
- Review portfolios and lesson/unit plans
- Recommend state certification or, if necessary, recommend termination, reassignment, or extension of student teaching experience

(Blair & Jones, 1998; Boreen, Johnson, Niday, & Potts, 2000)

❖ EFFECTIVE COMMUNICATION AND BUILDING RELATIONSHIPS

One of the keys to a successful student teaching practicum is effective communication. In fact, studies indicate that interpersonal communication is so important that it is considered to be a major factor in determining the effectiveness of co-teaching relationships (Dieker & Barnett, 1996; Thomas, Correa, & Morsink, 2001; West & Cannon, 1988). Similarly, Bruneau-Balderrama (1997) emphasizes the importance of "open and frequent communication" (p. 329) in the successful implementation of inclusion. The development of mutual understanding resulting from effective communication is equally important to a positive student teaching experience.

You cannot assume that you and your cooperating teacher are skilled at the communication process just because you are both nice people. Effective communication is an ongoing endeavor that takes conscious effort as well as considerable patience and maturity. According to Covey (1992), communication, or mutual understanding, "is a prerequisite to problem-solving and one of the most fundamental skills in life" (p. 138). Therefore, you must heighten your awareness of the words you speak, what message you intend to send, and how well you are understood (Knowles & Cole, 1996).

Developing Effective Communication Skills

Trust is equated with the confidence and integrity, commitment, and caring that are inherent in professionalism.

The need for you and your cooperating teacher to achieve an understanding regarding "the purposes, roles, and responsibilities during supervision is generally accepted in principle, yet it is hard to achieve" (McIntyre & Byrd, 1998, p. 412). A critical component necessary to develop this understanding with your cooperating teacher is **trust**. In fact, according to Williams (1989), trust is necessary in order to develop the positive interpersonal relationship with your cooperating teacher, your supervisor, and others that you need in order to receive approval and recognition.

Furthermore, development of trust takes a commitment of time and energy, but it is worth the effort. According to Covey (1992), "When trust is high, communication is easy, effortless, instantaneous, and accurate. When trust is low, communication is extremely difficult, exhausting, and ineffective" (p. 138). We acknowledge that communication is a shared responsibility. However, you can develop skills that will enable you to go a long way toward creating the sense of trust and openness you desire in a support relationship. These skills will be valuable in building effective relationships with your children and their families; these relationships will be discussed in Chapter 9.

Effective Communication and Nonverbal Behaviors

Research indicates that your **nonverbal behaviors** may enhance or impede the communication of your spoken language. This concept is particularly important when you consider that between 65% and 90% of all communication is transmitted nonverbally (Bowers & Flinders, 1990; Ornstein & Lasley, 2000; Thomas, Correa, & Morsink, 2001). In fact, nonverbal messages may represent the speaker's intent more accurately than her spoken words (Pugach & Johnson, 1995). Therefore, as you speak with your cooperating teacher and others you must be aware of what messages you are inadvertently sending with your body position, facial expression, and movements.

Nonverbal behaviors refer to the silent messages transmitted to others by body language.

For example, posture, gestures, intonation, and rate of speech can all enhance or impede the communication process. You may even want to have yourself videotaped as you communicate with children and teachers. Think about nonverbal communication signals and their possible implications such as the ones listed in the following Figure 3.1 as you observe yourself and others (Olsen & Fuller, 1998). Of course, you do not want to be in the position of second-guessing every movement; but increased awareness on your part can help prevent misunderstandings. Therefore, appropriate nonverbal behaviors can help you establish effective relationships.

In addition, you must be aware that nonverbal communication is symbolic in that it changes meaning depending on cultural experiences (Martin & Nakayama, 2000). Gestures and movements that are acceptable in one culture are taboo in another. Therefore, it is important to understand the cultural background of the children in your care and their families. These matters will be discussed later in the text.

Behavior	Implication
Leaning forward	Interest and cooperation
Arms folded across chest	Defensiveness or suspicion
Open or "steepled" hands	Cooperation and confidence
Picking or pinching flesh	Frustration or insecurity
Throat clearing; rapid speech	Frustration or nervousness
Chin stroking; tilted head	Evaluation or judgment
Coat unbuttoned	Cooperation and confidence

FIGURE 3.1   Nonverbal Communication Signals

Importance of Verbal Behaviors and Active Listening

Because language can be ambiguous at best, active listening skills are critical to the process of effective communication. The positive professional relationships you desire require that you achieve mutual understanding with others. Effective listening skill can serve as "a 'bridge' between the nonverbal and verbal forms of communication because it incorporates elements of both and affects both" (Thomas, Correa, & Morsink, 2001, p. 172). Therefore, active listening will improve interpersonal communication.

The following active listening skills will help you improve the quality of your communication as you listen carefully to what is being said. Each step does not have to be followed in each dialogue you have. However, you may find that through practice, you will use many of these skills automatically in your conversations.

Active listening skills generally encourage further communication. It has been said that we communicate who we are, and as individuals we differ markedly. Therefore, we should not be surprised that the words and phrases we use may become so distorted that the meanings we intend are not necessarily the messages that are received. Active listening is a valuable means of helping us achieve common understanding (Brill & Levine, 2002; Egan, 2002; O'Hair, Friedrich, Wiemann, & Wiemann, 1995; Olsen & Fuller, 2003).

You may think of yourself as a good listener. Perhaps you have never really thought about this. Reflect for a moment about how you would evaluate your own skills as a listener or as a communicator. The questions in the following Figure 3.2, adapted from O'Hair, Friedrich, Wieman, and Wieman (1995), may give you some insights.

You may find it interesting to have someone who knows you well rate you on these same items and compare the results. Your actual listening skills may differ from your perceived skills. You may have some listening skills that you

---

Active Listening Skills

- Respond by restating what you hear in your own words.

  "You are saying that . . ." or "You are feeling . . ."
- Clarify your understanding by requesting the speaker restate his words.

  "I'm confused about . . ." or "Let me try to explain what I think you are saying . . ."
- Check your perception of the speaker's feelings

  "Am I correct in thinking that you feel . . . about . . ."

(Adapted from Thomas, Correa, & Morsink, 2001)

As you answer these questions, respond with your initial reaction. Put a check in the box that most closely characterizes how you see yourself.

Statement	Yes	No	Unsure
1. People tell me that I am a good listener.	☑	☐	☐
2. I tend to interrupt people when they are speaking.	☐	☑	☐
3. I am good at letting people know that I understand what they are saying.	☐	☐	☑
4. I need to have information repeated.	☑	☐	☐
5. I can tell when people are really listening to me.	☑	☐	☐
6. I consider myself to be a good listener.	☑	☐	☐
7. I can remember what people are saying to me.	☑	☐	☐
8. My mind tends to wander when people are talking to me.	☑	☐	☐
9. I am a better listener in some situations than in others.	☑	☐	☐
10. I am good at asking questions when I don't understand what is being said.	☐	☑	☐

FIGURE 3.2   Listening Skills Self-Assessment

want to improve as you interact with others in a professional environment or you may be a better listener than you realized.

Another approach to developing effective communication is a behavioral model developed by Bergan (1977). This model can be used in conjunction with the active listening skills previously discussed. Bergan describes three dimensions of communication, the second of which includes five verbal prompts (Adapted from Kampwirth, 2003, p. 113):

1. Specification:"Tell me more about . . ."
2. Evaluation:"How do you feel about . . .?"
3. Inferences:"It seems to me . . ."
4. Summarizations:"Let's review my understanding of . . ."
5. Validation:"Can we conclude that . . .?"

Each of these prompts can be worded in question form in order to gather information and clarify understanding. Although the model was originally developed for behavioral consultation, it is useful for developing mutual understanding in many settings.

Even while you are engaging in dialogue, do not be afraid of silences in your conversation. Silences may indicate confusion or they may be opportunities for reflection. So, as you listen,"hear the silence, [and] observe the nonverbal responses" (Zachary, 2000, p. 27). Remember that active listening is also an attitude, not just a collection of scripted skills. It embodies a nonjudgmental desire to hear and understand, and it can lead to mutually supportive relationships.

❖ "GROWING PAINS": STAGES OF DEVELOPMENT

As you progress through your student teaching placement, you may find that your relationship with your cooperating teacher passes through several stages of development. As you progress through these stages, you will have opportunities to establish boundaries and to negotiate your responsibilities. Knowing the challenges other student teachers typically encounter may help you navigate through the exciting but often turbulent waters of your own experience.

Stages of Student Teaching

Stages of student teaching development have been a topic of interest since 1925 when Bagley first described seven distinct stages that focused on the student's performance of classroom tasks (Armentrout, 1927). Interest in this topic has continued throughout the last century; various authors have outlined three to seven stages (Piland & Anglin, 1993). For example, according to Schwebel, Schwebel, Schwebel, and Schwebel (1996), elements of the following four stages and characteristics are typically described by students in their journals:

- Stage 1: *The Early Days* may be somewhat overwhelming since so much information about children, teaching materials, and procedures must be absorbed in a short amount of time.
- Stage 2: *Becoming a Member of the Teaching Team* is a period of rising morale and establishing a sense of belonging to the class and the teaching team.
- Stage 3: *Soloing as a Teacher* is a time for solo teaching; morale may fluctuate, depending on feedback received from cooperating teachers, supervisors, and students.
- Stage 4: *Feeling Like a Teacher* is a settling-down period that focuses on working with the children and building confidence (pp. 23–26).

Interestingly enough, theories describing stages of development have been applied not only to student teachers but also to beginning teachers within the first three years of their careers. Both student teachers and beginning teachers share the same three stages of concerns that were originally described by Fuller and Brown (1975): *survival*, *task*, and *pupil*. During the *survival* phase, teachers and student teachers focus on issues of control and perception such as their ability to control classroom management and discipline and whether or not children and supervisors like them. During the *task* phase, their concerns primarily center on the work to be accomplished. For example, they focus on their own knowledge of appropriate teaching strategies, whether or not they have necessary materials and supplies, and their ability to manage time.

Finally, during the "pupil" phase, their concerns shift from their own performance to the well-being of others. They focus on the children's academic, emotional, and physical needs. This progression through stages of concerns is not linear; it has been described as overlapping, cyclical, and complex (Smith & Sanche, 1993; Martin, Chiodo, & Chang, 2001). As you progress through your own student teaching practicum, you will be asked to reflect on your own development as a teacher. You may consider where your own concerns fit into stage theory of teacher development. At some point on your way to "feeling like a teacher," you may discover that your concerns shift from being self-directed to being other-directed.

As you become more accustomed to your new teaching role, you may begin to feel a little pressured by fatigue and time constraints. However, you will benefit from taking a few moments to maintain contact with peers who are also navigating the turbulent highs and lows that accompany this adventure. The early childhood student teachers who meet as a peer support group often comment that it helps them to hear what others are experiencing. Some of their reflections may be helpful to you as well.

Comments During The Early Days

Students typically express a sense of exhaustion tempered with a desire to do more in the classroom. What are you feeling in the early weeks of your student teaching experience?

Comments on Becoming a Member of the Teaching Team

Generally, after a few days or few weeks, students express a sense of elation as they feel a sense of belonging. At the same time, they begin evaluating their environment and the people in it. If you are feeling a mixture of emotions right now, this is normal.

Comments on Soloing as a Teacher

This is the time period you have been anticipating throughout your months and/or years of preparation. The dream is that you will have a perfect experience in which your students demonstrate their learning. Furthermore, your children and their parents, your cooperating teacher, and college supervisor will appreciate your efforts. This is often true; but unfortunately, the reality is sometimes quite different. You may struggle with unexpected discipline issues or cooperating teachers who provide little or no feedback. Student teaching, like life, rarely follows the prescribed plan.

Comments on Feeling Like a Teacher

This is the phase in which you may feel like you are coasting through relatively calm waters. You may find yourself worrying less about your own success or failure. Tasks such as planning lessons and maintaining discipline

Voices of Reality: Student Teachers Speak

I am feeling slightly overwhelmed as I listen to conversations peppered with such alphabet soup ingredients as I.L.S., T.S.S., and O.D.D., and as I peruse the encyclopedia-sized curriculum that is to be in a mere 180 days, but I suppose that my current state of confusion is a normal part of this stage of the training process. . . . I feel like I'm becoming a hermit, kind of like "Shrek"! While my friends are out flitting around, I'm holed up in the quad, lounging around in my pj's at 7:00 in the evening. I'm having a severe energy drought."

Karla S.

I have a package at the post office that's been there for 3 days and I can't pick it up because I get home late! Right now I'm just worried about how long I'll be able to keep up this momentum and patience for teaching.

Keeley N.

I am anxious to start my "full-time." I can't wait to see my successes and failures. I am frustrated that I cannot help the kids with their personal life because of all their problems (divorce, violence, abuse, etc.).

Angie D.

Voices of Reality: Student Teachers Speak

I've been asking my co-op questions whenever possible, talking to her whenever the chance arises. Talking about personal life and family and things like that. The high point so far is just the relationship I have with my co-op and the other teachers around the school. Being trusted with the classroom/class at such an early time. After about 4–5 days, I was in the classroom with the students by myself, teaching.

Jamal D.

My co-op and I've been talking about teaching and our philosophy of teaching because we both know we'll only be teaching 10–15 years before a career change. We get along GREAT!! Our only issue is that we have a tendency to dress alike! On several occasions we've even worn the same color and outfit!

Keeley N.

I'm so fortunate to have this opportunity to work with and learn from this wonderful educator and friend. But sometimes she drives me absolutely, completely, bite-my-tongue, pull my hair out BONKERS!! I am the first to admit that I'm not exactly a natural "go-with-the-flow" gal. But—and I could very well be in error here—isn't there such a thing as excessive flexibility, as being too "loose"? Her "whatever" attitude makes me want to SCREAM at times!! AAHHHH!!!

Karla. S.

Voices of Reality: Student Teachers Speak

Well, let's just say these past 2 days have been frustrating. If I remember correctly, I'm supposed to have 2 weeks to myself to experience how teaching would be once I have my own classroom? But she was in the room more than ever, putting in her 2 cents while I was teaching. Finally, my supervisor talked to other co-ops. So today when I got in the room I heard her asking about her chair. She went out in the hall. Then she came back in and said she's been kicked out of the room. The teacher next door moved her chair and made her a place card at a table in the hall . . . She did not seem happy.

Rosa K.

There are occasions when my co-op will interrupt but she will always apologize for doing so.

Jamal D.

Free at last, free at last, thank the Lord, I'm free at last!! She actually did it; true to her word, she turned the classroom completely over to me and I had a fabulous time during these hours of independent professionalism! I received positive vibes right from the get-go as the students quietly (relatively speaking of course ☺) completed their activities.

Karla S.

become routinely manageable. Your focus may become more child-centered. In other words, you concern yourself primarily with helping each child learn and feel successful in your classroom. As one student phrased it during the final weeks of student teaching, "during our time together in the classroom, it's all about *them,* not about me." When you reach that point, you will know that you are indeed a real teacher.

❖ FINAL THOUGHTS

You may begin to breathe a little more easily as you consider the voices of other student teachers in relation to your own experiences. Therefore, your mixed feelings are normal as you navigate the turbulent waters of your teaching career. In fact, Brookfield (1990) states the following:

> Teaching is the educational equivalent of white-water rafting. Periods of apparent calm are interspersed with sudden frenetic turbulence. Boredom alternates with excitement, reflection with action. As we successfully negotiate rapids fraught with danger, we feel a sense of self-confident exhilaration. As we start downstream after capsizing, our self-confidence is shaken and we are awash in self-doubt. All teachers sooner or later capsize, and all teachers worth their salt regularly ask themselves whether or not they are doing the right thing. (p. 2)

Voices of Reality: Student Teachers Speak

I realized that my students see me as another teacher in their class. Although they know that I'm technically still a student, I receive the same respect as my co-op. The students will give me notes from parents (even though addressed to my co-op) and say "My mom said I should give this to my teacher."

Keeley N.

I'm discovering that the children are often the best "stop watches" for a lesson; it's really nonproductive to push them beyond their attentive capacities just for the sake of completing an activity as planned.

Karla S.

I am beginning to feel like a "real teacher." Some of the parents approach me and share insights or things their sons/daughters said. For example, "Mary thinks you are a great teacher and she loves that you are in her class."

Jamal D.

Although Brookfield's work is directed toward the teaching of adults in higher education classrooms, his perspectives of the teaching-learning process apply equally well to students and cooperating teachers in early childhood settings. Therefore, if you feel yourself capsizing from time to time, perhaps you should consider that mishap to be an opportunity for reflection and learning.

ACTIVITIES FOR REFLECTION AND ACTION

1. Keep an anecdotal communication log. Note a time when you feel good about the communication between you and your cooperating teacher. Note a time when you think the communication could be improved. Reflect on the verbal and nonverbal communication strategies employed in each instance.

2. As you progress through your semester, try to decide where you fit into each of the four stages of student teaching: Stage 1: *The Early Days,* Stage 2: *Becoming a Member of the Team,* Stage 3: *Soloing as a Teacher,* and Stage 4: *Feeling Like a Teacher.* Do you spend more time in one stage than another? Do you complete all four stages? What examples can you think of from your experiences that determine your current stage? Perhaps you would label the stages differently. You may wish to develop your own descriptors for the stages you experience.

 To Analyze some mini-cases and take some practice quizzes related to the content of this chapter, log on to the Companion Website at www.prenhall.com/tyminski. Go to Chapter 3 and choose from the links in the left column.

CHAPTER 4

Guiding Young Children in the Classroom

One looks back with appreciation to the brilliant teachers, but with gratitude to those who touched our human feelings. The curriculum is so much necessary raw material, but warmth is the vital element for the growing plant and for the soul of the child.

Carl Gustov Jung

Carl Jung's sentiments relate well to a discussion of classroom management and discipline. The young children whose lives you touch will remember whether or not they believe you cared about them much more than the perfect lesson you taught or the beautiful visual aide you spent hours creating. The learning environment you create will speak to your children. Is it warm and inviting? Is it aesthetically pleasing? Does it contain child-centered organized spaces accessible to all children, including those with special needs? Equally important, do you create a safe learning climate that communicates your concern for each child entrusted into your care? Your ability to develop supportive relationships with your children will enable you to guide individual and group behavior constructively. Although the curriculum, the instruction, and the planning skills are important, you must create a climate of warmth in which the soul of your young children can flourish. Only by touching their human feelings can you impact their lives in profound ways.

Metaphorical Perspective

Many student teachers desire their classrooms to be a warm, nurturing environment characterized by mutual respect, a sense of caring, and friendship. Then they encounter the reality of excitable, potentially disruptive young children. Frequently, these students may alter the student teacher's perspective from that of a nurturing caregiver to that of a custodial controller

Voices of Reality: Student Teachers Speak

When I think of my class, I think of twenty happy little springs tightly coiled, ready to unwind and start bouncing all over the room if I let my guard down even a little. I'm having fun though!

Angie D.

I am concerned about not having control of the class. Sometimes, especially in the afternoon, I feel like this is a zoo, and I am a zookeeper. But I want them to respect me and also see me as their friend.

Jamal D.

(Weinstein, Woolfolk, Dittmeier, & Shanker, 1994). As you progress through your student teaching, you may want to consider the metaphors you use to describe your children and your role as student teacher. For example, do you view yourself as a circus ringmaster, a guard, a parent? How do the metaphors you use reflect your approach to classroom management and discipline?

❖ EMPHASIS ON CLASSROOM MANAGEMENT

Classroom management is usually an area of concern for student teachers. Teachers are expected to be good classroom managers. Administrators, parents, and others may equate good teaching with good classroom management. In fact, you may be tempted to judge your ability to be a good teacher by your skills in the area of classroom management alone. Thus, the significance of this topic cannot be downplayed.

How will you prevent disobedience? You may wonder what you will do, for example, if a student tells you "no" or "shut up" or worse. How will you manage all the little details inherent in the daily schedules of young children? Are you adept at multitasking? Can you keep track of daily classroom routines, including nonacademic tasks such as attendance, snack and/or lunch routine, specials such as art/music/library/computer lab/physical education, as well as regularly scheduled support services such as speech/language therapy for children with special needs? Scheduling alone becomes a challenge. Then, on top of that, you must keep transitions short and smooth so that little if any time is lost, plan and carry out creative activities that meet the needs of all children, keep everyone on task, and manage to make sure that everyone cooperates pleasantly with few if any disruptions. If you think this is a challenge, you are correct. Do not be overly concerned, however. This is a challenge you can manage and enjoy!

Voices of Reality: Student Teachers Speak

From being a cheerleader, we use different voices to cheer and get attention. This is also a key to attention and alertness in the classroom. I also use the clapping rhythm, and they are attentive to that. They all listen and respect me. I am on my way to success! Sometimes I think teaching is like cheerleading.

Jackson L.

You will find your own style of classroom management. You may not be a cheerleader like Jackson L. or a zookeeper like Jamal D., but you will discover strategies that work for you as you learn to guide children's behavior and manage their environment.

Distinct Areas of Classroom Management

Some differences exist among the various definitions of classroom management. Generally, however, classroom management includes both preventative and reactive measures a teacher uses to create an environment in which effective teaching and learning can take place (Duke, 1987). People commonly think of a well-managed classroom as one in which children cooperate with the teacher and conduct themselves appropriately (Brophy, 1988). However, Machado and Botnarescue (2001) favor a more comprehensive definition that includes five separate areas: "(1) the physical arrangement of the classroom(s); (2) curriculum choices; (3) time management; (4) managing classroom routines; and (5) the guidance function" (p. 183).

For our purposes, we will address these areas in reverse order. We will begin by discussing guidance and discipline since this will probably be an area of immediate concern to you, at least initially. Next, we will address classroom routines and time management since these are areas of concern for many student teachers. We will address curriculum choices and physical arrangement of the room last since those are areas you will probably have little control over as a student teacher.

❖ DISCIPLINE AND GUIDANCE

Teachers have reported that misbehavior by individual children is their primary cause of job-related stress (Feitler & Tokar, 1992). They may judge their own effectiveness by the degree of cooperation they receive in their classrooms. The absence of misconduct, however, does not guarantee effective professional practice.

Definition of Terms

The term *discipline* is commonly defined as whatever teachers do to help children behave in an acceptable manner in school (Charles, 1996, 2002). Unfortunately, "whatever teachers do" is often viewed as punishment to force children's obedience. Yes, punishment may cause children to obey, but it can also teach disturbing lessons about the use of power (Clewett, 1988; Gartrell, 1995; Kohn, 1996; NAEYC, 1998).

In contrast, a more humane and perhaps more effective approach to behavior management stems from the derivation of the word *discipline.* Consider that it "comes from the same root as disciple, and the implication is that to discipline is to guide and teach" (Betz, 1994, p. 14). Knowing the derivation of the word may help focus your thoughts on guidance rather than on punishment as you develop your own philosophy of discipline.

One of the questions you will inevitably be asked when you interview for a teaching position is, "What is your philosophy of discipline or behavior management?" You should have at least a tentative response to that question in your mind right now as you observe and assume more and more teaching responsibilities. You may find it helpful to consider your answers to several questions as you formulate your philosophy. Reflecting on these questions and talking with your cooperating teacher and college supervisor will help you articulate your own approach to behavior management.

Guidance Approach

If our starting point for discussion is the root of the word *discipline,* then we should adopt a guidance approach to teaching children in a positive manner. This guidance approach develops from observing your children, knowing your children, and understanding the developmental levels of your children. The value of careful observation or kid-watching has been docu-

---

Sample Questions to Guide Goal Development

- What is the purpose of discipline?
- What does effective discipline look like? Feel like?
- Do you believe that children are innately "good" or "bad"?
- Do you believe that children are innately motivated?
- What is your attitude concerning conflict?
- How should problems between children or between children and adults be solved?

mented repeatedly as a means to meet children's developmental needs (Beaty, 2002; Flicker & Hoffman, 2002; Nicholson & Shipstead, 2002).

As you observe, you may want to consider the following questions adapted from Nelson, Erwin, and Duffy (1998b):

- How can I help this child feel capable?
- How can I help this child feel a sense of belonging and significance?
- How can I help this child learn respect, cooperation, and problem-solving skills?
- How can I get into this child's world and understand his developmental process?
- How can I use problems as opportunities for learning—for both this child and me? (p. 181)

Focus on the Child

Notice that the focus of these questions is the child. We are reflecting on what is best for the child's development rather than what will enhance your performance as a teacher. This is an important change in focus for most student teachers at a time when they want to shine and perform at their best.

Individual guidance talks with a child are a positive way to reduce mistaken behavior. You can talk about your expectations as you teach appropriate skills.

Teaching Self-Discipline

Gartrell (2002) recommends replacing discipline with a comprehensive guidance approach in order "to reduce mistaken behavior by holding developmentally appropriate expectations for children and by teaching democratic life skills" (p. 36). The goal of discipline then is teaching the child to regulate her own behavior. Brazelton (2001) provides an example of appropriate responses to a child's biting when at age one the child bites a caregiver and at age two the child bites a friend. In both instances, this behavior may be characterized as exploratory behavior typical of the developmental ages. When teachers or parents either ignore the behavior or overreact, the child will continue biting "as if to say, 'I'm out of control. Help me!'" (p. 40). This situation provides a teachable moment for guidance. The child may be receptive to learning a replacement behavior when she feels the urge to bite. Brazelton (2001) gives examples of suggesting to the child that she bite a "lovey" or even a rubber dog bone instead. The rubber dog bone may seem a bit insensitive, depending on your attitude about teaching a child to bite a bone like a dog; but the general concept of replacement behaviors is a helpful one. The child at age three needs help setting limits. Reminders and patient repetition are appropriate. You may find that a child, by age three, needs to be removed calmly from an excitable situation, reassured, and given a positive time-out.

Use and Misuse of Time-Outs

A time-out should not be punitive. It should not be lengthy. A rule of thumb is that the number of minutes of time-out should be no more than the child's age (Henniger, 2002; Porter, 1999). It should be a positive opportunity for the child to cool off, calm down, and gain control of her behavior (Crosser, 2005; Jones & Jones, 2004; Kyle & Rogien, 2004).

The child can even choose to go to a time-out area of the room when she feels herself losing control; similarly, she can choose to return to the group when she feels in control again. The time-out area need not be a dark, dingy corner. It may be an attractive place where a child may have a sense of privacy (Fields & Boesser, 2002; Nelson, Erwin, & Duffy, 1998a). Some teachers have an area in their room or in a nearby area in the building called the "chill out" space, the quiet place, or the "office" (Crosser, 2005).

As strange as it may sound, time-out can be positive. It does not have to be used as a punishment associated with behavior modification techniques. In order for a time-out to be positive, there must also be a time-in in which you provide the guidance and instruction the child needs to choose appropriate behaviors (Crosser, 2005; Kyle & Rogien, 2004).

In addition, you must model the behaviors you want children to emulate. For example, you may get tired or stressed from dealing with children whose temperaments cause difficulties from time to time. During these times, remember that children can sense your emotions; and they will be observing your behavior. You may have to model positive self-talk and restraint to remain calm when teaching children whose temperaments clash with your own.

One effective strategy to model for your children is the use of "I messages" (Gordon, 1974). Use of the pronoun "I" allows you to communicate your personal feelings about a behavior as well as an explanation as to why your feelings are important. For example, one child interrupts you when you are reading a story to the class. You can say, "I get frustrated when you interrupt me as I am reading aloud. You distract the other children, and they cannot listen to the story." This process allows you to identify your feelings and guide the child to understand the effect of her behavior on others.

As you are learning to use "I" messages effectively, you may wish to practice stating your feelings by using a formula. The three basic parts of this formula are as follows (adapted from Gordon, 1974):

1. **I feel** . . . (happy, sad, frustrated, etc.)
2. **when you** . . . (interrupt, yell, call out, etc.)
3. **because** . . . (I cannot hear others, children cannot listen to the story, etc.).

This is a skill that you can use in your professional life as well as in your personal life to confront your feelings about a person's troubling behavior in a nonjudgmental manner. Activities at the end of the chapter provide opportunities for you to practice giving and receiving "I" messages.

At the same time, you also need to focus on the feelings of the children in your care. As Faber and Mazlish (1982) emphasize, children "need to have their feelings accepted and respected" (p. 27). That does not mean, however, that you must accept the actions that go along with those feelings. For example, if one child hits another, you can tell her that you see how angry she is. Then you can tell her to use her words, not her fists to say what she wants. You are giving a name to the child's feeling; you are also providing her with guidance (Faber & Mazlish, 1982).

Behavior as Communication

Children communicate to us through their behavior. If you know your children, you can use the message they are communicating to discover their needs and feelings. Then you will be able to choose appropriate guidance strategies for each child.

Some of these behaviors are indicators of serious problems. If you have reason to believe a child may be in potential harm, then discuss your concerns with your cooperating teacher. As the NAEYC Code of Ethical Conduct indicates, you have a professional obligation to be an advocate for young

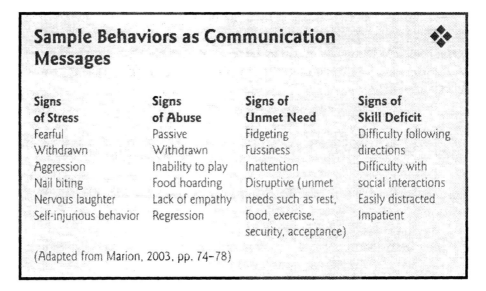

Sample Behaviors as Communication Messages

Signs of Stress	Signs of Abuse	Signs of Unmet Need	Signs of Skill Deficit
Fearful	Passive	Fidgeting	Difficulty following
Withdrawn	Withdrawn	Fussiness	directions
Aggression	Inability to play	Inattention	Difficulty with
Nail biting	Food hoarding	Disruptive (unmet	social interactions
Nervous laughter	Lack of empathy	needs such as rest,	Easily distracted
Self-injurious behavior	Regression	food, exercise,	Impatient
		security, acceptance)	

(Adapted from Marion, 2003, pp. 74–78)

children who cannot advocate for themselves. At the same time, you must be careful not to judge a situation too quickly. Your cooperating teacher's judgment and professional guidance will be invaluable in these matters.

❖ GUIDANCE STRATEGIES

The guidance approach to discipline involves teaching children social problem solving skills. Social skills are not innate. Children must be taught to share, to get along well with others, to name their feelings, and to handle anger appropriately. As young children learn these skills, there will inevitably be mistaken behaviors that provide teachable moments for the development of self-regulation.

Conflict Resolution

Although many models of conflict management exist, Gartrell (2002) recommends using a simple plan that he calls the "five-finger approach." This plan may be applied in both preschool and early primary settings.

The five-finger model can be used as part of the process during a number of guidance situations. For example, instead of the old-fashioned lecture *at* a child, this model can be part of a private guidance talk *with* a child. In a conversation with a child, you can encourage empathy for other people's feelings. You can also help him brainstorm other behavioral choices to use the next time a similar situation occurs (Gartrell, 2002).

Five-Finger Problem-Solving Model

- **Thumb: ("Cool off")** Calm down to set the stage for the process of mediation.
- **Pointer: ("Identify")** Children use words to identify the problem. Teacher may help as needed.
- **Tall guy: ("Brainstorm")** Children brainstorm ideas for problem solution. Teacher may help as needed.
- **Ringer: ("Go for it")** Children choose a solution to try.
- **Pinky: ("Follow-up")** Teacher monitors children as they try solution. Teacher may encourage and guide as needed.

(Adapted from Gartrell, 2002, p. 37)

Class Meetings

The five-finger model can also be part of the class meeting process. Class meetings have become customary in many primary grades, but older preschool children are not too young for class meetings, too. In fact, class meetings, sometimes called community meetings, are often encouraged as a means to reduce a young child's anxiety and provide a reassuring sense of belonging (McClurg, 1998).

Class or community meetings are an appropriate forum for encouraging children to develop problem-solving skills and self-regulation skills. Some teachers hold these meetings daily, others weekly. The frequency is not as important as the process, although regular meetings are recommended. Benefits include the following:

- Awareness of other people's perspectives, feelings, and experiences
- Development of empathy
- Self-awareness
- Empowerment of children
- Sense of inclusion rather than exclusion
- Consensus-making ability
- Development of positive social skills
- Development of listening skills
- Development of problem-solving skills

Guidelines have been suggested to maximize the benefits of effective meetings (Gartrell, 2002; McClurg, 1998; Styles, 2001). These are only guidelines; they can be adapted to meet the needs of your children and your teaching situation.

Guidelines for Class/Community Meetings

- Children and teacher sit in close circle
- Teacher's role: group member, coach when necessary. "secretary" function
- Agenda set by children
- Shared leadership of meeting
- Group members give and receive compliments or "appreciations"
- Five-finger problem-solving steps followed
- Questions for clarification
- Summarize choices made by consensus

From time to time, you will find young children whose problems are more serious than you or your cooperating teacher will be able to handle through positive guidance practices alone. These children may be facing serious life issues that you cannot fix. At these times, do not hesitate to ask for assistance. Part of your role as an early childhood educator is knowing when and how to be an advocate for the child and his family. A collaborative effort involving the child's family, senior staff, and support personnel such as mental health professionals and/or special educators may be necessary.

❖ ADDITIONAL BEHAVIOR MANAGEMENT TECHNIQUES

As you have observed in various field experiences prior to student teaching, a wide variety of behavior management strategies are being practiced. A few of the more common strategies will be described briefly in this chapter.

Assertive Discipline

This behavior management system has been used for over thirty years in early childhood level primary classrooms and with older children. It focuses on teachers' rights and children's rights. In other words, teachers have a right to require appropriate behavior from children; and children have a right to learn in a disruption-free environment. Teachers must be consistent, specific in their expectations, and provide clear, predetermined consequences. Teachers also use "I" messages such as "I like the way you raised your hand and waited to be called on" or "I don't like it when you run in this room" (Canter, 1976; Canter & Canter, 1992).

Although it can be effective, this approach has come under attack by critics who suggest that "it ignores methods for improving the quality of instruction and discourages the teacher from examining the specific classroom events that may be involved in the child's challenging behaviors" (Newcomer, 2003, p. 273). Even so, assertive discipline strategies allow the teacher to communicate positive behavioral expectations in a specific manner. An assertive teacher also knows exactly what appropriate consequences she will provide for inappropriate behavior in order to maximize her influence. She is in control (Canter, 1976).

Logical Consequences

The concept of logical consequences was developed by Rudolph Dreikurs, an Austrian psychiatrist. Dreikurs considers logical consequences to be the reasonable results of any behavior. The child's action must make sense in terms of the adult's reaction (Charles, 1996). The logical consequences must be developed cooperatively with the children and must be applied consistently. Accordingly, children choose the consequences of their appropriate or inappropriate behaviors (Newcomer, 2003). For example, a child who throws sand at the sand table center will be allowed to play somewhere else so that the other children will be safe. She will not be sent to a time-out chair to think about what she has done wrong because that would be a form of punishment.

Dreikurs maintained that children generally misbehave for four reasons: to get attention, to get power, to get revenge, or to withdraw (Machado & Botnarescue, 2001; Porter, 1999). Through careful observation of the child's reaction to being corrected, you can generally identify the child's goal. For example, a child whose goal is attention may snap her fingers and wave her arm in the air over and over. You can choose to ignore or extinguish the behavior. She may increase her finger snapping for a while before reducing the behavior and stopping it. You must be prepared to continue ignoring the behavior and not get discouraged (Martin & Pear, 1999).

A child whose goal is power may become confrontational when corrected. One whose goal is revenge may become hostile or aggressive. If a child feels inadequate or hopeless, her goal may be withdrawal. You can often prevent undesirable behaviors by giving children choices, by making your expectations specific and clear, and by having children participate in developing the rules and their logical consequences (Machado & Botnarescue, 2001).

Glasser's Choice Theory

William Glasser is a psychiatrist whose early work includes *Reality Therapy* (1965) and *Schools without Failure* (1969). He placed importance on the idea that people are rational beings who can control their behavioral choices.

Children can be taught to behave in a responsible manner that reflects society's standards. Accordingly, teachers must help children make appropriate choices by suggesting alternatives if the child cannot do so for himself (Glasser, 1986). In his later writings, Glasser changed his focus from control to choice, for example, *Choice Theory in the Classroom* (1988) and *Choice Theory: A New Psychology of Personal Freedom* (1998). Glasser's approach hinges on the belief that everyone has four equally important needs in addition to the basic need for survival:

- Need for belonging
- Need for power
- Need for freedom
- Need for fun

Glasser believes these needs are so strong that we will behave in such a way to have these needs met. He promotes the use of cooperative learning groups of no more than five students. These groups should be heterogeneous and changed periodically by the teacher. Children will develop a sense of belonging; the strong can help the weak; the children can make choices; and they will enjoy the process of learning together. Glasser calls this process positive interdependence (Glasser, 1988).

Limits or Class Rules

All effective teachers have a set of limits or classroom rules that they believe are essential. These rules may vary somewhat from teacher to teacher, but generally they are few in number, four to six; and they are stated in positive rather than negative terms. They are usually posted and visible. If the children are too young to read, the rules may consist of pictures.

Your cooperating teacher will have already established her limits with the children before you assume teaching responsibilities. Generally, you will be continuing the management policies she has put in place. Even so, the children are likely to test you to see if your limits are truly the same as your cooperating teacher's. You may need to give frequent reminders, however, before they accept these limits from you. Student teachers often feel torn between their desire to be liked and their desire to have good classroom management.

Behavior Modification

Although the term *behavior modification* sometimes has a negative connotation, we all use behavior modification techniques to some extent. For example, we may clap a rhythm or flick the lights in a room to get everyone's attention. When we look at a child and smile, we are actually practicing principles of behavior modification.

Proponents of behavior modification call our attention to critical aspects of good teaching such as the nature of teacher-child interactions, proximity, transitions, and reinforcement. Perhaps the most critical aspect of behavior modification is the positive feedback or constructive feedback that you give children. All children want attention. If they do not get it for appropriate behavior, they will get it any way they can. Research indicates that "effective behavior managers tally a 5:1:0 ratio of positive to corrective to negative feedback" (Newcomer, 2003, p. 254). Generally, you should give four to five times more social approval as social disapproval (Madsen & Madsen, 1974). That is why some teachers make a point of catching children being good. The social approval you use may be as simple as a smile, a nod, a glance, or a pat on the shoulder. This positive attention is usually a strong reinforcement for children.

Another aspect of behavior management involves the use of proximity and withitness. You need to be moving throughout the room, aware of what each child is doing at all times. Your proximity allows you to give children verbal and nonverbal feedback continually. Some cooperating teachers will actually draw a diagram of your movements throughout the room to help you see where you spend most of your time. This is helpful in determining if you are circulating throughout the room or staying in one place too long.

What to Do When All Else Fails

There will be occasions when all your best plans do not work out as you wish. You tried "Plan A" and "Plan B"; your guidance efforts did not work, and perhaps you already tried positive and corrective feedback. Now what?

This is the time to call for assistance. When you have a child who is not responding to the typical behavior management approaches already discussed, then you should speak up and ask for suggestions before she creates a dangerous situation for herself and others. A team approach works best. Involve the child's family, an administrator, support personnel such as a mental health or behavior specialist, a social worker, and anyone else that you and your cooperating teacher believe would be appropriate. Time is of the essence. A meeting should be arranged as soon as possible. Describe the child's behavior in specific terms, and describe what you have tried and the results. The team can then brainstorm alternative approaches and appoint an objective person to observe the child.

In some cases, you may need to have a crisis intervention plan in place. This is a written plan developed by the team that states what should be done, by whom, and under what circumstances if the child creates a situation potentially dangerous to herself or others. All parties of the team, including the child's family, reach consensus.

You may think you do not need something as drastic as a crisis plan for children in the early childhood years; but unfortunately, occasions arise when it is necessary. One cooperating teacher and student teacher reported the following event during the college supervisor's visit. It occurred in rural Pennsylvania, but the same situation could have happened anywhere. Picture this:

Place:	A primary class of twenty-two children ages 6 and 7. One cooperating teacher and one student teacher.
When:	Early spring day. After lunch and brief outdoor recess. No unusual or precipitating events.
Who:	Child B, age 7, recently diagnosed as bipolar, with a history of defiant behavior. Placed on medications by local physician.
What:	Class returns from recess and told to get ready for math lesson. Child B refuses to sit down. Runs toward floor-to-ceiling bookcase and begins climbing shelves and throwing books off shelves.
Act:	Activate Crisis Intervention Plan. (a) Student teacher immediately removes other children from room and takes them to designated area. Cooperating teacher uses phone in room to call for immediate assistance, remains with child B, tries to talk calmly and reassuringly with child B. Child climbs down. (b) Administrator arrives. Parent of Child B arrives. Child removed to medical facility for reevaluation of medications.
Next:	Child B returned to school with support of part-time teaching support staff (TSS) person.

The situations you encounter may not be as drastic as this one. Nevertheless, be prepared in advance with a back-up plan, seek assistance from a team if necessary, and develop a crisis intervention plan if appropriate. No one expects you or your cooperating teacher to have all the answers.

❖ REAL-LIFE ETHICAL DILEMMAS

Unfortunately, as you proceed through your student teaching experiences, you or someone you know may encounter an ethical dilemma regarding classroom management and discipline. How you handle these difficult situations and the lessons you learn from them will be important to your professional development. The following scenario is an actual, true-life story of a student teacher who recently found herself in the awkward position of wanting to please the cooperating teacher from whom she needed a positive evaluation and wanting to do the right thing for a young child. She turned to her college supervisor for help. As you read the scenario, you may want to refer to the NAEYC Code of Ethical Conduct. See Appendix 1.

Setting the Stage

Miss A. is a student teacher in a second-grade classroom of a suburban school district. She has only been in her placement for three weeks during fall semester. She gets along well with Mrs. B., her cooperating teacher, who is a well-respected teacher with twelve years' experience. When Miss A.'s college supervisor, Dr. R., makes her regular visits to the room for an observation and conference, she routinely asks how things are going. This time, the student's reply is disturbing. Think about what you would do in this situation.

Student Teacher's Response

Miss A. relates the following:

> All the children in this class are really great . . . except this one . . . J. At first, I thought he was charming. He always wanted to be near me. But now that I've been here awhile, I see that he is manipulative. We keep his desk separated from the rest because he is always disrupting the class. He chatters all the time, and he laughs inappropriately for no reason . . . He demands immediate attention. When he doesn't get his way, he steals or lies or destroys the property of other children. I could go on and on . . . . Mrs. B. has started locking him in the closet for time-outs. Yesterday, he was in there for forty minutes, and he wouldn't stop sticking his fingers out from under the door to bother the other children in the room. I'm not sure what to do. I'm not comfortable with having a seven-year-old locked in a dark closet at all, especially for a long time like forty minutes. He has been in there three days so far this week for anywhere from ten minutes to thirty or forty minutes. I don't think that's the right thing to do, but I don't want to get my co-op mad at me either. I feel like I have to choose between my co-op and the child.

College Supervisor's Response

After the formal observation of the student teacher's lesson, the college supervisor decided to stay longer to observe the children and return later for a three-way conference with both the student teacher and the cooperating teacher. The cooperating teacher's comments and discussion of the dilemma stem from that conference.

Cooperating Teacher's Response

> I'm pulling my hair out with J. I've tried everything I can think of. Time-outs help for a little while, but I don't think he really cares about anything. He won't work for tangible rewards; he doesn't care if he loses his recess. In fact, I think he likes staying inside with me . . . then I end up being the one who gets punished. Praise doesn't phase him; in fact, it makes him worse. None of the other children want anything to do with him, and they've tried to be his friend. His schoolwork is below grade level although his test scores show he can do the work if he wants to. . . . He has been in five foster homes since birth. This latest foster mother wanted to adopt him, but now she's not so sure. She has to pick him up every day at my door because the school won't allow him to ride the bus anymore. I genuinely like the kid; he can be sweet. In fact, when no other second grade teacher wanted him this year, I volunteered. I had him last year when I taught first grade so I knew him and the family already.

Ethical Dilemmas and the Decision-Making Process

The college supervisor had several ethical factors to consider. To complicate matters, the college needed to maintain a good rapport with the cooperating teacher and the school so they would take student teachers in the future. This became a teachable moment. Somehow, there had to be a positive outcome for the child, the child's family, the student teacher, the cooperating teacher, and the college supervisor.

When in doubt about how to handle an ethical dilemma, look to the NAEYC Code of Ethical Conduct as a guide for reflection to help you think through a course of action (Greenberg, 1999). The college supervisor relied on the principles stated in the Code of Ethical Conduct as the basis for guiding the discussion. Several parts of *Section I: Ethical Responsibilities to Children* were particularly helpful. For example, P-1.1 says that above all else, we must do no harm to children. That includes anything that is degrading, disrespectful, and potentially emotionally damaging. P-1.2 says that we must not discriminate against any child for a number of listed reasons, including the child's ability and behavior. P-1.3 says that when we make decisions about a child, we must involve all people who have relevant knowledge about that child. Without going any further, the Code of Ethical Conduct provided the supervisor with a clear mandate that the child's well-being was more important than any other concern. Clearly, the child's days of closeted time-outs had to end.

Through active listening and nonjudgmental conversation with both the cooperating teacher and the student teacher, the college supervisor helped achieve consensus on the following:

- Child J. should not go back in the closet at all, even for a brief period.
- Team conference with family and school support staff should be scheduled as soon as possible.

- Since both the cooperating teacher and the student teacher are in the room, one or the other should focus on child J. if he becomes a distraction so that the other children can continue their activities.
- Positive feedback should be given privately and discretely since public praise is ineffective. Avoid punishment.
- Guidance talks should be done privately, individually, and discretely.

Comments

The child's welfare had to come first. This was nonnegotiable. The student teacher was correct in bringing the situation to the attention of the college supervisor. The three-way conference provided an opportunity to brainstorm ideas for the future. It was not a forum to criticize what had already been done. These ideas became a starting point for focusing on the child, to help him regulate his own behavior.

As you would expect, this was an ongoing process that continued long after Miss A. finished her student teaching. The good news is that life improved for child J. The team met and recommended further evaluation. Child J. was eventually diagnosed with reactive attachment disorder (RAD) and began receiving therapy. He gradually responded to the teacher's repeated efforts to form attachments with him. Discrete positive feedback, private guidance talks, and avoidance of punishment all began to pay off.

In such cases, understanding *why* a child behaves in a certain way and participating as a *team* member to solve problems make a big difference. Whenever you are tempted to say, "I just don't *like* that child," then stop and tell yourself that the child who is most difficult to love is the one who needs your love the most.

❖ THE SUPPORT GROUP MEETS

Behavior management issues are frequently discussed during the support group meetings of the early childhood student teachers. Some concerns centered on how to handle sensitive discipline issues. Some of these students' shared thoughts may sound familiar to you as well.

As a result of student teachers' increasing awareness of the inappropriate behavior children are exposed to in their own homes and in their communities, the group discussion became emotion filled and reflective.

Do not, however, think for a moment that all students' experiences were negative. For example, other students shared stories that were quite different. Perhaps you can relate to these comments.

Voices of Reality: Student Teachers Speak

My low point of student teaching so far is feeling helpless when these young children come to school with their backgrounds . . . the divorce rate, the violence, the exposure to sex, etc. No wonder they have problems in school!

Angie D.

Yesterday. It was just a bad day. A day that you question how much we can really do as teachers. One child was refusing to participate in the "drug lesson" because "My mom does drugs; I know what they do."

Keeley N.

We had to remove a little girl from the "house activity area" today. She was play-acting having sex. Imagine . . . a four-year old!! I didn't know what to do. We didn't let her go back into the tent. After they left for the day, we took the tent down.

Jasmine L.

Voices of Reality: Student Teachers Speak

I haven't really run into many discipline issues, beyond the ordinary. No one is really openly defiant. They all seem sorry and apologetic when they do something wrong. To me, that's really important!

Krista U.

My co-op said, "Teachers don't smile until January." She explained to me that it is much easier to do it this way, rather than trying to enforce rules after none were set high from the beginning. This made sense for me.

Ruth H.

There have been numerous situations when we would both say the same student's name at the same time. They would just go back to their seat. After a few minutes then whichever teacher sent them back will go and talk to the student to make sure that they knew why they were sent back. I am not having any real problems so far.

Nancy F.

❖ FINAL THOUGHTS

Even when you feel a bit tired or discouraged, you may find that the simplest things will make all your efforts seem worthwhile:

> One of my girls picked a flower and brought it into me this morning. It's amazing how a near-weed can brighten a morning when received from a child.
>
> Krista U.

ACTIVITIES FOR REFLECTION AND ACTION

1. What is your cooperating teacher's philosophy of behavior management? List three key elements of her approach to discipline.
2. Write a statement that describes your personal philosophy of behavior management. Include a plan of action concerning what you will do if a child misbehaves repeatedly. What will you do first, second, third, and so on? At what point will you involve the child's family?
3. Describe a behavior incident involving one of your children. List two different ways to respond to this incident depending on your philosophy of behavior management.
4. As you reflect on your growth as a teacher, what insights have you gained about creating and maintaining a positive learning climate?
5. List the classroom rules you think are the most important to have in your classroom. What will be the consequence if these rules are not followed the first time? The second time, and so on?
6. Practice using "I messages" to express your feelings in each of the following scenarios. Refer to the pattern discussed in the chapter for guidance if you need it. You may wish to work with a partner so that you can give and receive feedback. You may also create your own scenarios for further practice.
   a. Mrs. X., your cooperating teacher, has been unusually silent all day. She has not given you any feedback on the lesson you taught this morning.
   b. The paraprofessional in your classroom complains to you about your cooperating teacher.
   c. A parent tells you that the school policy about not having holiday parties is ridiculous.
   d. Your cooperating teacher always seems to step in and give her opinion while you are teaching a lesson.

   To analyze some mini-cases and take some practice quizzes related to the content of this chapter, log on to the Companion Website at www.prenhall.com/tyminski. Go to Chapter 4 and choose from the links in the left column.

CHAPTER 5

Classroom Management: Environments and Routines

In searching for the fundamental principles of the science of teaching, I find few axioms as indisputable as are the first principles of mathematics. One of these is this, He is the best teacher who makes the best use of his own time and that of his pupils. For time is all that is given by God in which to do the work of improvement.

Emma Hart Willard

You have a limited amount of time to make a difference in the lives of young children. What you do in the relatively brief period children are with you can have a lasting impact. Therefore, you must carefully plan the classroom routines you implement, the transitions you use to move children from one activity to another, and the overall environment you create. When children enter your room, do they feel safe, respected, accepted, and celebrated for their uniqueness? Is your room a place for dreaming and laughter as well as learning? How well do you use the gift of time to do the work of improving the young lives entrusted to you? The answers to these questions will help you fulfill your commitment to honor the children in your care (Turner, 2000). Perhaps you can relate to following the words of a student teacher in the peer support group.

You too will find your own ways of communicating to children that you care about them. The physical environment will also communicate to children that their emotional needs will be met in this place. Therefore, you need to give careful thought to how you will manage the physical space of your classroom.

❖ PHYSICAL SPACE AND CLASSROOM MANAGEMENT

One important aspect of the physical environment is aesthetic appeal. The ideal early childhood learning environment will have an inviting, homey atmosphere. Color, materials, and furniture are important factors in creating the sense that your room is a wonderful, safe, caring place (Feeney, Christensen, & Moravcik, 2001; Hendrick, 2003). As a student teacher, you will be able to affect the aesthetics of the environment as you create learning stations, bulletin boards, and interest centers. At the same time, safety must always be an important concern when planning the physical environment. Consider the following factors as you plan.

Safety and the Classroom Environment

The physical environment in the classroom should be one in which children are safe from harm at all times. The arrangement of items in the room may be predetermined by your cooperating teacher. However, you can still do some troubleshooting. For example, you can closely examine the environment for potential threats to child safety. The following questions for classroom safety assessment may help guide you (adapted from Branscombe, Castle, Dorsey, Surbeck, & Taylor, 2003):

- Are there any electrical cords that may trip children?
- Are there any electrical cords that children can pull?
- Are all electrical outlets equipped with safety covers?
- Are there any appliances plugged in that may attract the attention of inquisitive children?
- Are there any rough or sharp edges on tables and counters that could hurt a child?
- Are all floor surfaces free from spilled water?
- Do floor coverings have safety grip backings to prevent slipping?

You may be able to add to this list of safety assessment questions as you examine your classroom.

You may also find it helpful to get down on the children's level as you make your safety check. There may be potential threats to safety that you cannot see from an adult perspective, such as loose screws or splintered wood underneath furniture.

Color and the Classroom Environment

The study of the psychology of color is controversial at best. Even without the benefit of scientific research, some people insist that color can affect the mood and overall tone of a physical space. They suggest use of bright colors such as red or orange for active play areas and muted colors such as shades of blue or green for quiet activity or rest areas. You may want to experiment with colors as you designate various activity centers of your room and decide for yourself what, if any, effects color has on the psychological climate of the area. Use of colors and decorative artwork is frequently suggested in order to create a sense of beauty and emotional well-being in children's environments (Cruickshank, Jenkins, & Metcalf, 2003; Feeney, Christensen, & Moravcik, 2001). Just be sure to display items at children's eye-level, not at yours.

Texture and the Classroom Environment

Some children are sensitive to the feel of materials such as hard, soft, and coarse. For example, in the quiet areas such as the book corner, place large soft pillows and soft carpeting. In the blocks area or painting area, use harder surfaces on flooring. Children enjoy using their senses to explore their environments, so give them the opportunity to play with sand, water, and sandpaper-covered letters and numbers. You can help preschool children

---

Example of Texture Activity

1. Collect a variety of materials cut in approximately the same size and shape so that the only identification clues will be tactile. Suggestions include velvet, vinyl, burlap, silk, corduroy, and fake fur.
2. Blindfold child, have her close her eyes tightly, or put materials in bag so that they cannot be identified by sight.
3. Have child use words to describe how each sample feels. Children may work in pairs or with an adult.

(Adapted from Schirrmacher, 2002)

make a texture book containing fabrics and materials of various textures. Texture books also offer opportunities to stimulate conversation. You can use any number of items, including material collected on nature walks, to stimulate language development and exploratory activities.

Furniture and the Classroom Environment

When possible, you can have an area in your room that contains comfortable home furnishings such as a chairs or a sofa with soft pillows. Even a soft rug with big pillows will provide an inviting area for children to enjoy story books. Some teachers set up aquariums with fish or small pets, areas for listening to soothing music, and quiet areas for children who need to take a break from busy group activities (Branscombe, Castle, Dorsey, Surbeck, & Taylor, 2003). This type of planning leads to a sense of physical security in your classroom (Whitehead & Ginsberg, 1999).

Multicultural Elements and the Classroom Environment

Display nonstereotypical posters, photographs, artwork, and artifacts of people representing various ethnic and racial backgrounds. Integrate displays with picture books and story books that also show children and adults in a

The physical environment in your classroom can help create a climate of safety and emotional security that encourages learning.

positive light. Children will benefit from learning about their own culture and that of others on a continuing basis. This topic will be discussed at greater depth in Chapter 9.

Arrangement of Physical Environment and Program Philosophy

Physical space in early childhood rooms is often arranged in conjunction with program philosophy. For example, if you prefer a teacher-centered approach, you may choose to have a separate desk for each child with your desk being a center of attention. The author cautions, however, that many teaching professionals, including the author, indicate a preference for child-centered physical environments.

If you also prefer a child-centered approach, you may choose round tables or clusters of desks to encourage collaboration by cooperative groups of children; your desk may be tucked away in a corner (Brewer, 2001). A project approach, typically seen in the preschool programs of Reggio Emilia, may require spaces for discovery purposes as well as a special space called the *atelier*. The atelier contains materials for children to make visual recordings documenting their learning experiences (Henniger, 2002). Thus, you can sometimes determine the philosophic approach of a particular program by the arrangement of the physical environment. This is something for you to consider carefully. When the time comes for you to go on job interviews, prospective employers often ask how you would arrange your classroom.

Common Types of Physical Space

You can expect to see various types of physical space designated in early childhood rooms. Of course, there will be variations depending on the age and needs of the children and the goals of the program. The following list, suggested by Davis, Kilgo, Gamel-McCormick (1998), is fairly typical:

- Space for gross motor play activities
- Space for fine motor activities requiring tables
- Space for large group activities
- Space requiring a water source
- Space for each child's personal belongings
- Space for teacher materials
- Space to store materials and consumable supplies
- Space for parent or family member conferences and information

A number of considerations may guide your decisions about arrangement of space. Some of these considerations may be beyond your control, such as size and location of your room in the building. Nevertheless, a few guidelines may be helpful (Dodge & Colker, 2000).

Guidelines for Use of Available Space

- Use shelves or furniture to define separate areas so children focus on activities with few outside distractions.
- Keep noisy areas close together such as blocks and large toys.
- Keep quiet areas close together such as books and puzzles.
- Place interest areas close to resources such as painting areas near a water source.
- Store children's supplies in a separate area from teacher's supplies.
- Arrange traffic pattern to minimize interruptions and to allow access for children with special needs.
- Arrange interest areas so that you can see all children at all times.

You may have only limited opportunities to influence the physical space of the room during your practicum. However, your cooperating teacher may allow you to decorate an activity center or re-arrange some of the furniture for a time. Keep in mind that you should try to create a place that *all* children and their families will feel "is already made for me, both snug and wide open, with a doorway never needing to be closed" (Morrison, 1998, p. 12).

Classroom arrangements that are child-centered allow children to work and play safely at all times. There are areas designated for specific purposes.

❖ EMOTIONAL CLIMATE AND CLASSROOM MANAGEMENT

You can help create a safe, caring, emotional climate in your room by doing several simple things each day. Each child in your care deserves a good beginning to her day. You can be at the door to greet children when they arrive. This may also be an opportunity to encourage positive communication with family members who drop off children in the morning. You may learn if some event in the child's life may impact her behavior during her day with you. Similarly, each child deserves a good ending to her day. Perhaps you can share information with families who arrive as you say good-bye to each child (Feeney, Christensen, & Moravcik, 2001).

Despite your best efforts, there may be events that impact young children's lives in a negative manner. At those times, you may have to ask for assistance from your cooperating teacher and support personnel. Sometimes, you can help children work through fears as they play.

Young Children and Fear

Young children can be affected by events even though they do not yet have the language to express their fears. In fact, these children tend to generalize their fears to other people and situations more readily than do older children. This can lead to increased distress as they believe the adults in their world can no longer protect them from danger (Jackson, 1997).

Children are often exposed to images of war and terrorist attacks on television. Even if children do not see the news, they are frequently exposed to

---

Ways to Nurture a Positive Emotional Climate

- Give each child some individual attention each day.
- Display children's projects and work products.
- Model the behavior of calling attention to children's achievements and encourage them to praise each other.
- Allow children to make appropriate choices.
- Include elements of children's cultural identity into daily lessons.
- Demonstrate appreciation of children's families by inviting them to participate in activities.

(Adapted from Gestwicki, 1999)

images in various forms of media that frighten them. This fear may manifest itself in behavioral changes as they play or draw.

Using Play to Develop Emotional Well-Being

In your early childhood environment, you may be able to help children "transform their play from acting out violence into imagining a more comforting and secure resolution" (Levin, 2003, p. 73). You can provide props that will allow them to create safe endings to their play scenarios. Also, do not be afraid to talk with children about disturbing news events. For example, watch their play and ask "why" questions. You can lead them to tell you what they already know about a topic such as war or terrorists. Children may be looking for reassurance that they are safe and protected. They may not ask you for more detailed information than they already have.

If you believe, however, that a child's fears require intervention from a specialist, talk to your cooperating teacher about your concerns. Some schools and centers have play therapists as members of the support staff team. Play therapy is actually derived from the work of Carl Rogers on client-centered therapy in the early part of the twentieth century. Often, children engage in unstructured play in a room filled with specially selected toys and materials. A therapist observes, engages the child in conversation, and helps the child discover solutions to problems (Warner & Sower, 2005).

Classroom Management and Rules

Children's behavior and discipline have been addressed in Chapter 4, but establishment of classroom rules is something you should consider as you plan the overall management of your program. Creating a positive tone with your class rules will contribute to the overall emotional climate of your room.

General recommendations are that rules should be few in number. They should be simple. They should be worded positively. They should be clearly defined and displayed somewhere in the room. They should also be applied consistently (Slavin, 2000; Warner & Sower, 2005). For younger children, picture cues may accompany each rule. Many teachers believe that children should participate in the development of the rules so that they have greater "buy-in" to living by the rules they helped create (Kyle & Rogien, 2004). Notice the class rules in the classroom that you visit. Do they follow the general guidelines suggested here?

Posting simple, positively stated rules is not enough. You need to have discussions with your children about what each rule means. For example, if a rule says, "Respect other people's property," then children need to discuss what that means. Children can provide examples of how they can respect property.

In addition, if you have particular rules of behavior that you need children to follow while you are student teaching, you need to discuss those with your cooperating teacher and with the children. For example, you may have a different tolerance for noise levels and movement during play and work time than your cooperating teacher. Children can generally adapt to different expectations of behavior around different people.

❖ CLASSROOM ROUTINES

Management of classroom routines is another important element of creating a positive learning climate. Children feel a sense of security in an environment in which routines are well established. Indeed, for some children, the greatest stability in their volatile lives is the predictability of their daily routines away from home. Research indicates that having a schedule and following it consistently significantly increases children's sense of security and reduces stress, even in young children (Hamner & Turner, 1996). That is not to say that flexibility is harmful, but predictability is reassuring (Honig, 1996).

Therefore, while you are observing your cooperating teacher, be extremely aware of the daily routines. Take notes if necessary. Some cooperating teachers do not mind if you make changes. Others are quite particular about having routines kept exactly the same way because they do not want to have to reteach procedures to the children after you are gone. In any case, check with your cooperating teacher first before making any changes.

Daily Routines

Whether you are teaching infants, preschoolers, or children in the primary grades, the arrival and departure routines are important. The arrival period must be handled in such a way as to make a smooth transition from the child's home. This should be a friendly, relaxed time in which each child is greeted and parents may wish to share information with you. Depending on the age of the child, there will be consistent, daily routines of diapering/toileting, circle time, snack/meals, clean-up, learning stations, instructional time, individual and group play, and rest/nap times. Departure routines are equally significant in order to provide a sense of closure. Departure provides you with an opportunity to share information with each child's family, either in person or by some other means such as a sharing journal. Sometimes, this informal, daily communication can be more effective than a formal conference (Warner & Sower, 2005).

In order for you to appreciate the importance of routines in the children's lives, think about your own life and the routines to which you have become

Reflect on Routines in Your Life

- What morning routines do you have in your daily life? Evening routines? Exercise routines? Recreation routines? Driving routines?
- What purpose do you think these routines serve?
- How do you feel if something prevents you from carrying out your planned routines?
- What is it about your routines that you like?
- What routines have you implemented in children's lives? Why?

accustomed. The preceeding questions, adapted from Feeney, Christensen, and Moravcik (2001), may be helpful.

Even though routines are important in early childhood programs, you still have the flexibility to make some changes. For example, if children are engaged in an activity that is totally absorbing their attention, you may elect to extend the activity longer. If you must eliminate or shorten another activity, then you may tell the children what the change in routine will be and why.

❖ TIME MANAGEMENT

Time management is one of the important aspects of classroom management. For some student teachers, adhering to a schedule or monitoring the pace of lessons and activities is difficult at times. For example, you may plan activities that you think will be challenging and take considerable time only to find that children breeze through them without difficulty. Other activities that you thought would be simple need more time because you did not anticipate misunderstandings. Occasionally, you may forget to watch the clock in order to draw activities to a close at the scheduled time, particularly if you are absorbed in teaching a lesson you have spent hours preparing. Do not despair, however, since **pacing** is something that generally improves with experience.

Pacing refers to time spent on each portion of the lesson such that children neither feel rushed nor bored waiting for others to finish.

Schedule for Managing Classroom Time

While you are having your practicum experience, you will have minimal opportunity to organize a schedule for your children. For now, it is more than likely already organized by your cooperating teacher within certain restrictions set by the school or center regarding meal time or recreation space shared with others. Even so, place close attention to how blocks of time are organized for your children's developmental age. Every program may make

Sample Schedule for All-Day Kindergarten

8:00–8:45	**Free Choice Center Activity at Centers**
8:45–9:15	**Opening, Daily Calendar, and Morning Messages**
	Active involvement of children with morning song, calendar and weather, and daily schedule
9:15–9:45	**Shared Story Time with Teacher**
	Teacher reading with a Big Book, a predictive story, or a story reflecting a particular theme
9:45–10:15	**Emergent Literacy Activity**
	Teacher may model thinking aloud and writing with marker some thoughts and drawing picture to illustrate some words
	Children have time to write in their journals while teacher encourages and coaches
10:15–10:45	**Recess/Snack**
	Snack may relate to story read earlier such as theme about apples
10:45–11:45	**Assigned Centers**
	Centers may be designed around a particular theme such as a recent visit to an apple orchard
11:45–12:15	**Lunch**
12:15–1:15	**Math**
	Math activity can revolve around theme such as making a class graph of favorite apple foods or colors
1:15–1:45	**Shared Writing: Language Experience Story**
	Children talk about recent field trip to apple orchard while teacher writes simple sentences they say aloud onto chart paper
	Sound-letter relationships and other beginning literacy skills are developed
1:45–2:15	**Outdoor physical activity**
	Children explore and use play equipment in kindergarten play area
2:25–2:45	**Center Activities: Children's Choice**
	Children have time to explore activities of their choice in centers that promote learning
2:45–3:00	**Daily Summary**
	Review days activities and prepare to go home

certain adaptations or accommodations for the interests and needs of its unique children. There are many variations. However, one sample schedule is provided here.

Schedules will vary due to the developmental levels of children and the goals of the program. However, Gestwicki (1999) suggests the following guidelines for development of good schedules:

- Predictability in sequence of activities throughout the day
- Flexibility to allow for special events or sudden changes in the weather
- Blocks of time for child-initiated activities as well as teacher-initiated activities
- Blocks of time for active experiences as well as passive experiences
- Variety of activities to allow for developmental differences in attention span and in abilities

These guidelines apply to classrooms in the primary grades also. Keep in mind that your daily schedule may be structured around certain nonnegotiable blocks of time allocated for lunch, recess, and special subject areas such as art, music, and physical education. These may be predetermined by an administrator. Although there are many variations, a sample primary grade schedule is shown here.

In the primary grades, there is increasing emphasis on academic subjects. You may receive guidance about how many minutes you should allow for daily reading and math instruction, for example. As a student teacher, you should follow the routine established by your cooperating teacher.

Sample Schedule for a Grade 3 Class

8:30–8:45	**Arrival, Opening, Attendance, Lunch Count** Children may also have a quiet, routine activity to complete during the arrival period such as a daily oral language exercise
8:45–9:00	**Class Meeting**
9:00–10:00	**Math**
10:00–11:30	**Reading**
11:30–11:45	**Spelling**
11:45–12:30	**Lunch and Recess**
12:30–12:40	**Read-Aloud, Sustained Silent Reading (SSR)** A chapter book may be read aloud to the whole class and/or children and adults may read books silently
12:40–1:30	**Writing Workshop**
1:30–2:15	**Science/Social Studies/Health** Subjects are taught on a three-week rotation cycle
2:15–2:50	**Specials: Art, Music, Library, Physical Education, Foreign Language**
2:50–3:20	**Centers: Student Choice** Interdisciplinary centers may be related to themes being taught in subject areas
3:20–3:30	**Closing, Homework, Clean-Up, and Dismissal**

Transitions

Transitions are also an important segment of classroom management for you to plan. Anytime you change activities or move children from one area of the room to another, you must consider how to make these transitions as orderly and brief as possible. You may find that many children become excitable and prone to creating disruptions during less structured times. Therefore, plan ahead.

Student teachers sometimes struggle with noninstructional or transition time. Research indicates that as much as one-fourth to one-third of the day can be lost due to transition times between activities (Newcomer, 2003). This unstructured time can be especially difficult for children with special needs such as attention deficit hyperactivity disorder (ADHD).

In order to minimize mistaken behaviors during transition times, you need to do careful planning. Some teacher tips include "using a color wheel to indicate a new activity, playing 'beat the clock', using transition buddies, and marking the end point of the transition with a fun or rewarding activity" (Newcomer, 2003, p. 255).

Lost time can be a management problem in all levels of early childhood education from nursery school through the primary grades. One surprising study found that as much as 35% of the nursery school day is spent transitioning from one activity to another (Berk, 1976). Consequently, observe how your cooperating teacher handles these activity changes without disruptions. You may discover that her methods work for you or you may want to be creative and try a few of your own. Guessing games or memory games can occupy children's minds and bodies while they are lining up and waiting to go to play outside. You may even want to solicit children's ideas as to how to make transitions smoother. They may be more cooperative in getting their coats on quickly if they have developed the solution to the problem themselves (Alger, 1984).

If you find that transition times are not as quick or smooth as you would like, then ask yourself the following questions:

- Have I given the children notice that a transition is coming? What signal(s) have I given?
- Do the children understand what is expected during each transition?
- Are my directions simple, clear, specific, and consistent?
- Have I allowed sufficient time for transitions? Too much time? Too little time?
- Do I need to allow for individual differences in the transition process?

As you gain experience and observe other teachers, you may collect your own bag of tricks or ideas to smooth transitions between activities. Creative ideas can help make transitions pleasant, productive times rather than stressful time-wasters.

Sample Ideas for Transitions

- Use transition buddies for children who have difficulty remembering transition procedures.
- Give a warning 5 minutes before transition time.
- Use a picture schedule for children as needed.
- Use music as transition cue.
- Use pretending, such as tiptoe like a quiet mouse.
- Name a color that children are wearing to indicate who may move to a location.
- Use gestures as a signal. For example, when children see your hand raised, they silently make the gesture until everyone has her hand raised.
- Use riddles or clues as transition cues.

Outdoor Physical Environment

Another equally important component of management to consider is children's use of outside areas. Regular outdoor experiences are readily acknowledged as an integral component of developmentally appropriate practice for children through age eight. These experiences require careful planning so as to maximize opportunities for development of gross motor skills as well as exploration of the natural environment (Bredekamp, 1987).

Young children benefit from outdoor play spaces that are created to simulate a home environment (Whitehead & Ginsberg, 1999). For example, gardens, shrubs, flowers, and vegetable gardens expose children to a variety of multisensory experiences. Both the context of the outdoor space and the design of the play facilities "engage and entice children's sense of inquiry, stimulates their imaginations, invite exploration, communicate a sense of belonging and cultural identity, and support their sense of developing competencies" (Debord, Hestenes, Moore, Cosco, & McGinnis, 2002, p. 33). Thus, a child-centered outdoor physical environment can enhance the development of the whole child.

❖ FINAL THOUGHTS

Many of the strategies you learn to apply to classroom management are preventative in nature. The procedures you establish with your children will indicate that "this is how we do things so everyone can work and play together safely." The positive emotional climate you create as well as the physical arrangement of the room will have much to say about your respect for each

Voices of Reality: Student Teachers Speak

I am using the clapping rhythm to get their attention. For the majority, they all listen and respect me as the "real" teacher. I know I am not the "real" teacher but I sure feel like it!

Jasmine L.

I will be doing full time on Monday. This is going to be a unit on pumpkins. I think I am well planned for it, but I am still worried about transitions or time-fillers. I will probably be over planned, but until I am done it, I will probably worry a little. I think it is different when it is not your room.

Nancy F.

Students respond so much better to rules and limits if they're made fun. We made paper airplanes and I immediately set the limits so that airplanes were not just flying through the air. But instead of just telling them to put them away, I told them air traffic control didn't clear them for take off so they had to fly over to their airports (a.k.a. backpacks) and stay parked. It seemed to work and I had no problems with them. It was just one of those spur-of-the-moment things but my co-op mentioned to me afterwards that she thought it made such a difference as opposed to simply listing rules.

Krista U.

child. Preplanning will prevent many difficulties concerning behavior or safety issues.

Watch closely how your cooperating teacher begins and ends each day, how she has children enter and exit the room, how she gets children's attention and transitions them from one activity or space to another. Notice routines that she has established for everyday activities such as bathroom use, getting a drink of water, asking for help, cleaning up, and putting away. These are all decisions you will be making when you are a professional early childhood teacher.

❖ ❖ ❖

ACTIVITIES FOR REFLECTION AND ACTION

1. Design a room arrangement for an early childhood grade or age group that you would like to teach. What do you think this room arrangement reveals about your philosophy of teaching?

2. What rules would you expect to see hanging in your own classroom? Write a list of five words, keeping in mind the guidelines listed in this chapter.

3. What can you see yourself doing to create a learning climate in which children feel safe and cared for?

To analyze some mini-cases and take some practice quizzes related to the content of this chapter, log on to www.prenhall.com/tyminski. Go to Chapter 5 and choose from the links in the left column.

CHAPTER 6

Observations and Evaluations of Student Teaching

To be a teacher in the right sense is to be a learner. Instruction begins when you, the teacher, learn from the learner, put yourself in his place so that you may understand what he understands and in the way he understands it.

Soren Kierkegaard

Kierkegaard's thoughts on being a teacher in the right sense underscore the importance of learning from your learners, no matter how young they may be. Your student teaching observations and evaluations provide you with unique opportunities for inquiry and collaboration. The feedback you receive will guide you in your process of reflection and self-analysis to maximize your opportunities to become a teacher in the right sense.

❖ MAKING THE MOST OF THE OBSERVATION/ EVALUATION PROCESS

Each student teacher's reactions to observations and evaluations may vary due to individual differences in experiences and temperament. After initial adjustments, however, most people find their own ways of positively responding to these opportunities for personal attention and assessment. A common reaction is for students to desire more rather than less feedback.

You may find that each of you discovers your own way to deal with your feelings during observations and assessments. The more you can focus on your children rather than on your observers, the better off you may be. Some experienced teachers will admit to having a case of the jitters when administrators or parents or even student teachers watch them.

Voices of Reality: Student Teachers Speak

My supervisor comes in all the time, so it's just normal to have her there. But I really just stay true to myself and be me when I'm observed. Yes, I do have a tendency to check myself and watch more closely what I do, but it doesn't change the way I teach. I guess it helps that I have a theater background so it's easy for me to stay me!

Keeley N.

I've had a lot of trouble with this! I think student teaching is so hard because you have people [co-op/supervisors] watching your every move. Being watched like that has made me nervous, and I tend to make mistakes.

Lauren C.

Just doing what I have planned and not looking at them is a big help. Many times there are other teachers in the classroom. The whole idea of it happening on a daily basis really plays a big role in the comfort level.

Jamal D.

All teachers receive formal, written feedback yearly. Although the forms vary, they generally contain information summarizing the lesson content and the teacher-child interactions, comments regarding the strengths observed, and suggestions concerning improvements or things to think about. This observation/evaluation and follow-up discussion process will be ongoing throughout your professional career since there is always room for improvement. As Asa Hilliard (1999) states, "Learning to be a teacher is a long-term process. . . . As teachers mature, experience, study, and reflection help develop their perspective . . . [which] is as necessary for teachers of young children as for teachers at the higher grades" (pp. 58–59). In addition, as a lifelong learner, you will be a role model for your children.

Goals of Observations

The goals of observations and follow-up discussions vary according to the assumptions on which good teaching is based. Generally you will find that your college supervisor, for example, will be interested in more than whether or not you are doing a good job. She may be inquiring about your concerns and questions as well as your personal reactions to your experiences (Rodgers & Dunn, 2000). In other words, the observation visits may be somewhat holistic in nature, centering on your overall well-being in addition to your teaching proficiency. Machado and Botnarescue (2001) list five goals of student teaching supervision that reflect this broad paradigm:

- To provide specific feedback based on valid assessments regarding performance
- To enable the exchange of ideas and suggestions that will improve skills
- To develop a positive attitude towards continuous self-improvement and inquiry
- To develop the practice of reflection and self-assessment
- To maintain the accepted standards of early childhood teaching practice

Climate of Trust

In any case, the intention is to create a relationship that fosters a climate of trust in which all parties can learn from each other. This perspective reflects the views of Caruso and Fawcett (1986), who propose a developmental approach that regards supervision as a reciprocal relationship between the early childhood professional and the supervisor so that they may learn from each other and influence each other as adult learners. This mutual learning opportunity is significant since the backgrounds of professionals in many early childhood programs vary widely.

❖ OBSERVATIONS OF TEACHING

When student teachers think of observation, the first mental picture is often that of a cooperating teacher and/or a college supervisor sitting in the back of a room with a clipboard writing notes. This is the most common practice but not the only means of observational data collection.

Direct Observation

The traditional approach to assessing student teacher competence is through some type of direct observation. The assumption here is that good teaching behaviors are objectively identifiable and measurable in multiple contexts (Danielson, 1996; Stodolsky, 1985).

In any event, when you are observed, your college supervisor will utilize a rating form of some type to record observations and make suggestions as a basis for discussion with you and your cooperating teacher. This approach has been criticized as a snapshot of performance on isolated occasions (Gellman, 1992–1993). Therefore, in order to get a better overall picture of your performance, college supervisors generally make an effort to observe you interact with children or teach different types of lessons at various times of the day.

Format

A clinical model of supervision by your college supervisor will generally entail five steps:

- **Preobservation conference.** The focus of the observation may be established. Your college supervisor may wish to take a look at your written lesson plan or goals. Because of scheduling concerns, however, this step is not always possible.
- **Observation.** Generally, an activity or a lesson is observed in its entirety so that transitions, introduction, and closure may be observed.
- **Summary and analysis.** A written record of teacher-child interactions, strengths, areas for improvement, and suggestions may be noted.
- **Postobservation conference.** Preferably, this will occur immediately following the observation. If not, then a time is usually arranged as soon as possible. This meeting may be two-way, you and your college supervisor, or three-way, you, your cooperating teacher, and your college supervisor.
- **Postobservation conference analysis.** Generally, you will be asked to reflect on what went well, what could stand improvement, as well as strategies to try in the future. In time, your self-analysis will be confirmed or you will be counseled concerning changes.

Purposes of the Observation

Observations can be a helpful means of receiving professional coaching and increasing your ability to self-assess. A variety of observation strategies may be helpful to you.

- **Tracking your movement.** An observer draws a sketch of the room that includes tables, desks, activity centers, and boards. The room may be roughly sectioned into quarters. Then the observer traces your movement with a pencil for a specified period of time. Later, when you examine the drawing, you will see if you circulate throughout the room or if you have a limited territory or power base from which you operate (Boreen, Johnson, Niday, & Potts, 2000; Henry, Beasley, & Brighton, 2002).
- **Gender discrimination.** Most student teachers blatantly deny any favoritism toward girls or boys. For example, you may be positive that you respond to the girls as often as the boys. How sure are you? Have an observer keep a list of each child in the room. Each time you respond to a child or initiate communication with a child, the observer can put a tally mark beside the child's name. At the end of a specified time period, you will see who had more of your attention, boys or girls. You will also notice if a few children monopolized your attention to the exclusion of others (Sadker & Sadker, 1994).

■ **Frequency of interaction:** In a room containing a multicultural mix of children, have an observer sketch a matrix. This matrix may use simple identifiers such as AM—Asian male, AF—Asian female, HM—Hispanic male, and so on. Then the observer may tally the number of interactions that occur between you and various children. After a period of time, you will be able to see clearly if any patterns emerge (Adams, Shea, Liston, & Deever, 1998).

The variations of purposes for observation are virtually endless. For example, you may benefit from having an observer look for the types of questions you ask, the positive or negative feedback you give, or the amount of wait time you allow various students after posing questions. The information you receive from these directed observations is extremely helpful in increasing your awareness of teacher behaviors that you may wish to continue or alter.

Informal Observations

In contrast, the observations conducted by your cooperating teacher are often less formal since she is with you on a daily basis. The two of you may share a dialogue journal that is passed back and forth as an opportunity to jot down questions, comments, and suggestions during your busy day; other teachers prefer to use their own system of index cards or sticky notes to communicate during the day. In other words, creativity and informality are common practice.

Nevertheless, no matter who conducts your student teaching observations, you may expect a discussion to be part of the follow-through process. Too many times, these discussions tend to be "dominated by cooperating teachers and student teachers take a passive role" (Guyton & McIntyre, 1990, p. 525). A lost opportunity for growth occurs when conferences focus solely on specific classroom events with little analysis of the teaching process in general.

Consequently, in order to maximize your satisfaction with the feedback you receive, you may need to initiate a conversation with your cooperating teacher rather than wait for her to do so. A useful practice is a guided reflection that involves asking four questions. They may be used alone, with a colleague, or, in your case, with your cooperating teacher. These questions, suggested by Hole and McEntee (1999), may be adapted to follow an observation in order to encourage dialogue and analysis:

■ Step One: What happened?
■ Step Two: Why did it happen?
■ Step Three: What might it mean?
■ Step Four: What are the implications for my practice? (pp. 34–35)

You can use this four-step process to reflect on events that occur randomly in our daily interactions with children. For example, the author observed Diane L. reading a story to a group of kindergarten children who were seated in a circle around her. Her story time was disrupted by a series of events beyond her control. She expressed displeasure with the way she handled the situation. Here is her use of the four-step process described above:

Step One: Outside, a late spring rain storm had been brewing for some time. The rain came and all of a sudden there was a loud clap of thunder, and a large streak of lightning appeared. One child jumped up and ran to the window, followed by a few others. Another child burst into tears. Others just sat there. But no one was paying any attention to me. So, I got up and closed the curtains and insisted that everyone come back to our rug so we could finish the story.

Step Two: I know that they are just naturally curious about everything. I also know that thunder and lightning can be frightening. So why did I feel I had to ignore their reactions and just get on with business? I knew I was making a mistake even as I closed the curtains, told them to be quiet and come sit back down.

Step Three: I think I felt I had to finish my activity with the children because I was being observed. I was afraid of appearing to lose control. I didn't know how to handle something so unexpected.

Step Four: In the future, I need to take care of children's immediate feelings. We needed to talk about thunder and lightning and answer their immediate questions. We also needed to talk about fears. This would have been a more important lesson than my read-aloud story any day.

Through this type of critical incident reflection, you can cultivate the skills you need to not only survive but also to thrive in the complex world of teaching young children.

Peer Coaching

Another form of direct observation that is gaining notice is peer evaluation during student teaching. This process is sometimes referred to as peer coaching. Students have been making observations of each other and giving feedback during early field experiences for years. Many studies have found peer coaching to be a valuable means of increasing collaboration and transferring knowledge from theory to practice (Anderson, 1998; Anderson & Radencich, 2001; Buttery & Weller, 1988; Hatch, 1993; Hudson, Miller, Salzberg, & Morgan, 1994). Rauch and Whittaker (1999) report findings from a study in which students utilized peer coaching during their student teaching semester. Each student chose a partner who was also student teaching. One formal observation with a written evaluation was required of each peer. Results suggest that students generally find coaching from a co-learner to be helpful, particularly when a postobservation conference is part of the process. It is suggested that, in order to be successful, this model of peer coaching must be "built on a preservice program that emphasizes collaborative experiences and reflective teaching in all education courses" (p. 75). If your college does not require peer observation and feedback, this may be an option to consider if you feel comfortable doing so. You may want to discuss this with your college supervisor and cooperating teacher to add another dimension to your experience.

Video Observations

College supervisors and cooperating teachers often suggest that you videotape yourself. Valuable information can be gleaned from observing yourself teaching formal lessons as well as interacting with children in less formal situations.

Before using this option, check with your administrator to see if there is any policy you need to know about regarding the use of a video camera in your room. Some parents do not want their children's picture taken for any purpose. This is something you need to check on before proceeding.

Often, student teachers feel self-conscious about using this observation tool. You can reduce the anxiety of being on camera by setting up the video camera in the room for several days before turning it on. That way, the children (and you) become used to its presence.

Some student teachers prefer to watch the tape alone. Others want their cooperating teacher's input. Regardless, you may find that observing the tapes gives you an "aha" moment. Tapes provide you with the distance you need to see mannerisms you may have been unaware of or classroom procedures that can be improved on. They also provide a record of exemplary teaching that you can incorporate into an electronic portfolio. Portfolios and their use will be discussed later in this chapter.

❖ EVALUATION

Generally, a discussion and analysis will follow your observations. You will have the chance to evaluate your own performance and to receive evaluative feedback. This is an opportunity for continual improvement. Probably, at no other point in your career will anyone pay so much attention to what you are

doing and care enough to provide you with both positive feedback and suggestions for improvement.

Receiving Criticism

None of us is perfect, not even master teachers. Expect to receive constructive criticism. How you deal with it is of paramount importance. Some observers are even urged to find something to write as a suggestion for
improvement, no matter how flawless the lesson appears.

Receiving constructive criticism is an art. You may be tempted to cry, leave
the room, get defensive, or argue. Do none of these. Denial, anger, and de-
pression are all counterproductive reactions. Remember that the person who
is giving you feedback genuinely wants you to succeed.

You can take several steps to turn negative feedback into a positive experience. If you do not understand, seek clarification. Try focusing on one thing
at a time. The following questions give you the idea of how the process works:

- What is the one thing I can adjust to make my instructions to the children clearer?
- What is the one thing I can change to make my classroom management better?
- What is the one thing I can change to make transitions smoother?

These kinds of questions give you the specific response you may need to
make positive changes. Questions such as these also indicate that you are
willing to seek help. Even if you do not agree with the message you hear,
thank the evaluator for his suggestion. Try it to see what happens. Even if a
particular suggestion does not work for you, at least you tried it; and you
will be perceived as someone who is receptive to new ideas.

Personal Characteristics

Although pedagogical knowledge and technical skill are important, a positive student teaching experience requires effective interpersonal communication skills. Hence, many teacher education programs assess professional
potential by evaluating students' personal and professional characteristics, social and emotional characteristics, and interaction and communication skills.
The following figure provides a sample form utilized by cooperating teachers and college supervisors to address these areas; self-evaluation by student teachers is also encouraged. In the opinion of some, these characteristics
and skills are important enough to be considered an eleventh competency
in addition to those based on the Interstate New Teacher Assessment and

---

Code: N–Not Observed **O**–Unsatisfactory **I**–Satisfactory **2**–Superior **3**–Exceptional

N   0   I   2   3   Personal and Professional Skills

        A. Meets obligations and deadlines by appropriate planning
        B. Follows guidelines, procedures, and rules
        C. Exhibits behaviors that reflect high professional standards
        D. Submits work products that reflect high professional standards
        E. Demonstrates effective use of problem-solving techniques
        F. Demonstrates tenacity and self-reliance in pursuit of solutions

N   0   I   2   3   Social and Emotional Characteristics

        A. Rapport with students
        B. Rapport with school personnel (includes all support staff)
        C. Displays appropriate affect and emotions
        D. Demonstrates awareness of social behaviors and expectations
        E. Demonstrates awareness of professional social behaviors and
           expectations
        F. Reflects on and takes responsibility for own behavior
        G. Accepts suggestions positively and modifies behavior appro-
           priately
        H. Demonstrates enthusiasm and a positive attitude
        I. Accepts the role of both positive and negative experiences in
           personal development
        J. Demonstrates ability to make the best of all experiences

N   0   I   2   3   Interaction and Communication Skills

        A. Demonstrates respect for the feelings, opinions, knowledge,
           and abilities of others
        B. Is empathetic with others
        C. Uses effective interpersonal skills
        D. Functions effectively in a variety of group roles
        E. Solicits and considers alternative viewpoints
        F. Communicates effectively with diverse audiences

FIGURE 6.I   Evaluation of Personal and Professional Characteristics

Support Consortium (INTASC) ten core standards (Blue, Boothby, Newell, O'Grady, Toro, & Tyminski, 2001).

Your heightened awareness of these somewhat subjective areas may help you in your ongoing reflection of your personal growth as you interact with children, parents, colleagues, and others in the community. You may also want to talk with your college supervisor to find out what observation/evaluation criteria she will use and compare her criteria to those in the preceding figure.

❖ SELF-EVALUATION

You are already aware by now that good teaching requires continual and thoughtful deliberation. Throughout your teacher education program, you have been asked to reflect on your learning and its implications for practice. During your student teaching experience, critical reflection provides an opportunity for self-evaluation that may take several forms, including writing journals and developing portfolios.

Reflective Journals

You may have been asked to respond to reflective journal assignments in various education courses. This is a common approach used by professors to encourage you to examine the beliefs and assumptions you already possess regarding teaching and learning. These assignments often help students become more receptive to new ideas (Carter, 1998).

Furthermore, reflective journals can be an effective tool for self-evaluation and improvement during student teaching. College supervisors often require that you maintain a daily log of some type, either in a notebook or in electronic form, in which you record daily events as well as your thoughts and reactions to those events. Sometimes this journal is for your eyes only; sometimes it is shared as a basis for dialogue between you and your supervisor or cooperating teacher.

Notwithstanding, the theoretical basis for a journal requirement is well grounded in the literature. The concepts of reflective thinking, reflexive inquiry, and reflective teaching have been the focus of attention for decades (Zeichner & Liston, 1996). For example, Dewey (1933) promoted reflective thinking as a necessary goal of education. He viewed it as an active process involving the deliberate consideration of beliefs and knowledge and the potential consequences of actions based on those beliefs and knowledge. Equally important, Schon (Jossey-Bass, 1983) recommended both formative and summative reflection of the teaching and learning process that he called reflection-in-action and reflection-on-action.

Forms of Inquiry

More recently, Cole and Knowles (2000) distinguished between two forms of inquiry that have different goals. As they explained, reflective inquiry is the process of examining teaching practices so that they may be improved; reflexive inquiry, on the other hand, is the process of examining personal histories or teaching autobiographies in order to understand the source of one's beliefs and assumptions. Both forms are valuable vehicles for understanding yourself as a teacher as you write in your journal or teaching log.

As a reflective teacher, you realize that you teach "students who live lives beyond the classroom walls, and schools and classrooms exist in settings that directly affect the type and quality of education that can occur" (Zeichner & Liston, 1996, p. 77). Therefore, your reflection should include a focus on the context as well as the content and manner of children's learning.

Process of Journal Writing

In any event, some students view journal writing as drudgery while others enjoy it as an outlet for personal expression. In order to facilitate the process, consider the possibility that the only rule in journal writing is that there are no rules. For example, writing lists and drawing sketches are just as acceptable as formal paragraphs. You may want to consider some of the topics suggested by Cole and Knowles (2000) to help you get started:

- Instances in your classroom that you identify as real learning
- Preconceptions or stereotypes that have been challenged or changed as a result of your experiences with students
- Relationships with colleagues
- Students with special needs
- Issues of gender, race, and class
- Working with parents
- Highlights of the day, week, or term
- Your professional development needs
- Your disconnections in teaching: the things that cause you grief, the things you do not understand
- Things about teaching that excite you (p. 60)

Sample Personal History Questions

- What importance did your family place on education? And what attitudes were expressed toward education by your family?
- How have your family's attitudes toward education influenced your current attitude and teaching practice?
- What critical incidents stand out in your life as a learner? How have they influenced your teaching practice today?

(Cole & Knowles, 2000)

Whether you share your journal with anyone or not, you may find that your writing provides a unique opportunity for self-evaluation and growth. Over time, the written reflections may become a vehicle for problem-solving and genuine communication that continue throughout your professional career.

Portfolios

Artifacts are concrete evidence of knowledge as well as the ability to demonstrate understanding of the knowledge and apply it in a meaningful way.

Another form of self-evaluation, portfolio development, may be considered an extension of the reflective journaling process (Yoo, 2001). Indeed, the use of reflective portfolios is becoming widespread. Children, even in the early childhood years, are capable of thinking about their work and choosing samples that showcase their progress. You are, in effect, doing the same thing when you select **artifacts** and write reflections to demonstrate your progress in meeting established criteria. Similarly, many schools are now expecting teachers to develop a portfolio that indicates their professional development as effective educators (Painter, 2001; Wolf, Whinery, & Hagerty, 1995). This self-evaluation tool has even been hailed as the most effective means for improving the teaching-learning process (Zubizarreta, 1994).

Your portfolio is a reflection of who you are as a teacher. You will keep it and modify it throughout the course of your career.

Definition of Terms

A portfolio has been defined in various ways. Ryan and Kuhs (1993) define it as a student's collection of work that shows progress toward specific, predetermined goals. However, Wolf (1996) cautions that it should be much more than merely "a miscellaneous collection of artifacts or an extended list of professional activities" (p. 34). He warns against portfolios characterized as either a scrapbook of meaningful mementos or a steamer containing large quantities of random artifacts (Wolf, 1996). Shulman (1998) offers a definition that delineates significant steps included in the process of portfolio creation:

> A teaching portfolio is the structured documentary history of a set of coached or mentored acts of teaching substantiated by samples of student work and fully realized only through reflective writing, deliberation, and serious conversation. (p. 37)

Equally important, portfolios are an active and interactive process. They have even been suggested as being a more accurate representation of teacher quality than either a direct observation or a high score on a paper and pencil test (Gellman, 1992–1993). Perhaps they do indeed have a more lasting impact on both the lives of teachers and their children than other assessment options (Lyons, 1999).

Levels of Portfolio Development

In any case, as a student teacher, you may still need to be concerned about two to three different levels of the portfolio development process: the working portfolio, the exit portfolio, and the interview portfolio (Dietz, 1995; Toro & Newell, 2001).

- The working portfolio, as its name implies, is a work in progress. It documents your growth toward the performance standards of your teacher education program; you may receive coaching or mentoring as needed throughout this process.
- The exit portfolio is also becoming an accepted rite of passage prior to graduation as you present evidence that you have mastered required teacher education competencies; often, a somewhat formal presentation involving conversation with interested faculty, peers, and others is part of the exit portfolio process.
- Finally, you will, in all likelihood, develop an interview portfolio that is a modified form of your exit portfolio. This is the portfolio you will take with you to your job interviews. It contains a resume and the highlights of your experience and teacher preparation activities that will sell you to a prospective employer.

Multimedia Portfolio Development

Furthermore, a relatively new approach to portfolio preparation is the e-portfolio or multimedia portfolio. Many students are developing a CD-ROM version of their paper-in-a-binder portfolio to hand to prospective employers. While you are completing your student teaching, you may want to keep this approach in mind. Typically, you will be collecting artifacts such as sample lesson plans, photographs of your bulletin boards, and photographs of you and your children engaged in various learning activities. You may also consider making video and audio clips as well as links to your own Web site that you can include in a compact disc. You can use this electronic format to demonstrate your creativity and your technology skill (Kilbane & McNergney, 1999). Yes, this is a time-consuming process, but many students believe it to be an asset when undergoing the all-important job search process.

In any case, whether you are preparing a paper-in-a-binder portfolio or a multimedia portfolio or both, you will be concerned about assessment of your work. Your portfolio will be unique in that it reflects your own experiences, perceptions, and personal choices.

Criteria for Assessment

Nevertheless, many teacher education programs use standardized criteria in order to establish consistency in the assessment of portfolio quality in what may be a somewhat subjective process (Smith et al., 2001). Students generally select performance categories such as those established by Danielson (1996):

- **Planning and preparation:**   Design of instruction and organization of content for children's learning
- **Classroom environment:**   Noninstructional interactions necessary for effective learning to occur
- **Instruction:**   Engagement of children in process of learning
- **Professional responsibilities:**   Professionalism and professional development

Then they develop their portfolios to indicate how they meet specific standards in each category.

When you create your own portfolio, you may include materials that showcase your personality as well as your teaching skills. You may assemble a product that contains many of the following:

- One or more examples of your best lesson plans and units
- Instructional materials that you prepared yourself
- Photographs of children playing or working at various centers that you created

- Photographs of bulletin boards you have created
- Photos or diagrams of ways you have organized your classroom
- Written evaluations of your teaching that you are particularly proud of
- Samples of children's work
- Certificates of attendance at a workshop or conference
- Your resume
- A statement of your philosophy of teaching young children

No matter what products or artifacts you gather for your portfolio, the important thing to remember is the written reflection of WHY you are choosing to include each one. What does each item reveal about you as a successful early childhood student teacher who is meeting the standards for entry into this profession?

Regardless of what standards and categories you select, your portfolio should indicate that you are a reflective practitioner. At some point, whether in portfolio conversations with professors or in interviews with prospective employers, you must take ownership of your portfolio as an authentic representation of who you are as both a teacher and a learner. Accordingly, it documents your willingness to be a lifelong learner who closely observes and understands children, who assesses herself and develops goals for continual improvement, who learns through inquiry, and who collaborates with others (Yoo, 2001).

❖ STATE STANDARDS AND HIGH-STAKES ASSESSMENT

According to a poll conducted in May 2002 for the Educational Testing Service (ETS), 93% of the respondents endorsed testing teachers on their knowledge of teaching skills and knowledge of subject matter; and 90% favored teacher training programs to prepare highly qualified teachers (Perkins-Gough, 2002).

Praxis Tests

In order to meet the demand for testing of teacher candidates, the ETS has developed a series of Praxis examinations. These examinations are perhaps the ultimate in high-stakes assessment for future teachers. The consequences of passing these examinations have a direct influence on your ability to obtain the teaching positions you desire. According to testimony of Patty McAllister, Executive Director of State and Federal Regulations at ETS, the Praxis Series have a 50-year history of use in the United States. The examinations are now administered in all 50 states, six times a year at 650 test sites. They are continually updated to reflect the current knowledge of technology, pedagogical knowledge, and practice expected of qualified teachers (McAllister, 2003). The results of these tests affect licensure decisions. The specific Praxis test requirements vary from state to state. Therefore, you must investigate the particular requirements not only for the state in which you are completing your teacher education program but also the requirements for any states in which you think you might wish to seek employment.

Passing the Praxis Tests

To help you pass the examinations, you may obtain study guides prepared by the ETS. You may also check your state Department of Education Web site. For example, Pennsylvania's Department of Education offers samples of various Praxis tests online. Beginning in the fall of 2003, a Diagnostic Preparation Program is available from ETS to help you plan a course of study to prepare for the examinations. In addition, check out the ETS Web site (www.ets.org) to explore test preparation options.

ETS will also grant testing accommodations for the Praxis series if you have appropriate documentation of a disability such as a specific learning disability or a visual impairment. The ETS Web site contains further information concerning the types of documentation necessary as well as the procedure for obtaining accommodations. If you are accustomed to receiving extra time on tests or testing in a separate room, for example, you may have these same accommodations for the Praxis series if you follow the specified procedures for requesting these accommodations.

Certification

As you complete your student teaching, start considering where you would like to teach if you have not done so already. To help you in your planning, be aware that many states have reciprocity agreements that accept other states' certification requirements. There is a National Association of State Directors of Teacher Education and Certification (NASDTEC) contract to help educators who move to other states. Approximately forty-eight jurisdictions, including the District of Columbia, Guam, and Puerto Rico, have signed the current NASDTEC Interstate Contract allowing appropriately trained personnel to transfer their certifications to other locations. Requirements regarding experience may vary; so, to be safe, check with the Department of Education in each location you are considering. Each jurisdiction has its own office of certification and licensure that may impose special requirements to be fulfilled within a reasonable time period (Goethals & Howard, 2000; NASDTEC, 2002).

❖ PEER SUPPORT GROUP

Early in the semester and even during your weeks of full-time teaching, teaching observations and assessment can become issues of concern. Later, as the semester rolls to an end, one of the topics of frequent discussion is the often-required portfolio presentation and its ensuing evaluation. The following thoughts shared by the peer support group may give some insights regarding their experiences as well as yours.

Evaluations and the Unexpected

Student teachers quickly realize that flexibility is one of the qualities they must develop if they do not already possess it in abundance. On a daily basis and sometimes on an hourly basis, the unexpected can be expected to occur. Student teachers have been known to remark that one of the few things predictable about children is their unpredictability; occasionally, they find the same to be true about their cooperating teachers and their college supervisors.

Time Management

A common complaint from the peer support group seemed to focus on too much to do, not enough time. Student teaching, as you know, becomes all consuming. Then, as graduation looms ahead, you realize that not only do

Voices of Reality: Student Teachers Speak

My supervisor arrived at 8:55 this morning to observe me teach language arts. The 9:00 "pop" fire drill reminded me of the tremendous need for flexibility, for accepting the unexpected. I didn't allow myself to dwell on the fact that my reading lesson would just have to wait until Monday, and instead focused my attention on the next lesson, a "following directions culinary activity." I was SO happy with this experience! The throne of flexibility will probably not bear my buttprint anytime soon. But I firmly believe that I have made remarkable strides in this respect . . . . I feel as though I am becoming well equipped to adapt to the never-ending surprises that pop up each day in the classroom. But, isn't there such a thing as excessive flexibility, as being too loose?

Karla S.

Today was okay. Not too eventful. My supervisor came in for a surprise visit which I thought wasn't supposed to happen until November, but it was no big deal. My lesson wasn't earth-shattering but it went OK. The high point of my day was keeping my cool when she came in. I was glad she wasn't here yesterday when someone threw up in class!

Paula M.

Voices of Reality: Student Teachers Speak

This whole portfolio thing has me really stressed out! I don't know when I'm supposed to have time to finish it while I'm student teaching. I want to do a CD for my interviews but I just don't have time to prepare everything right now. How are we supposed to student teach, finish a portfolio, and begin filling out applications for teaching positions?

Angie D.

I'm going to concentrate on finishing my paper portfolio right now. And after graduation, I'll have time to burn CD's to hand out. The only thing I'm worried about is making the presentation—the questions I'll get. I'm going to practice ahead of time. I also want to do mine on the last day so I can see what other people's portfolios look like.

Lauren C.

Actually, I'm looking forward to the whole presentation thing. I want to tell everyone what I've been doing, and I'll have a captive audience! I'm not worried. The portfolio is part of who I am.

Keeley N.

you have to compete for a professional teaching position, but you also have one or two important tasks to complete before graduation. For many students, the prospect of portfolio presentations and/or portfolio conversations is a reality that can be stressful. Even the preparation of the portfolios themselves can get out of hand as some students spend excessive money, time, and energy to prepare attractive binders or multimedia presentations (Wheeler, 1996). This is not necessary. Even with limited resources, high quality, professional-looking portfolios are quite do-able.

❖ FINAL THOUGHTS

You have learned by now that teaching is an exceedingly complex blend of art and science. Danielson (1996) claims that "a teacher makes over 3,000 nontrivial decisions daily. It is useful then to think of teaching as similar to not one but several other professions, combining the skills of business management, human relations, and theater arts" (p. 2). It is no wonder then that student teaching is not too soon to develop the habits and skills of observation, reflective analysis, and collaboration with peers that will guide your development as a lifelong learner. Throughout your professional career, you will probably participate in direct observation, journal writing, professional conversations, and portfolio development. Becoming a skilled professional takes time and the courage to take risks. As Dewey (1902/1959) wrote, "It involves reaching out of the mind" (p. 95). Accordingly, the ability to think outside the box sometimes requires a transformation, the development of new habits of the mind through connections or mentoring with others (Freidus, 1996).

ACTIVITIES FOR REFLECTION AND ACTION

1. All student teachers get observed and assessed in various ways as a learning experience. In teacher evaluation, there must be some vision of what good teaching is. What is your vision of good teaching? How will you know when you are a good teacher?

2. Observe your cooperating teacher and make notes to review later. Pay attention to her classroom routines. How does she start a lesson or activity? How does she give directions? How does she motivate children? What is the sequence of the steps for a lesson? How many minutes does she spend on each step? What questions does she ask? How does she know if the children understand? How does she handle misbehavior? How does she allow for differences in ability? How does she close the lesson? How do the children react to the lesson? Then, reflect on what you have observed. What would you do the same or different? What questions do you have for your cooperating teacher?

To analyze some mini-cases and take some practice quizzes related to the content of this chapter, log on to the Companion Website at www.prenhall.com/tyminski. Go to Chapter 6 and choose from the links in the left column.

CHAPTER 7

Assessment of Young Children

To teachers, students are the end products. All else is a means. Hence there is but one interpretation of high standards in teaching: standards are highest where the maximum number of students—slow learners and fast learners alike—develop to their maximal capacity.

Joseph Seidlin

These words are particularly relevant in the education of children today. Terms such as *high-stakes testing, assessment,* and *accountability* have become controversial. Debates ensue over the necessity of assessing young children. Parents and teachers question not only the need for assessing young children but also the manner in which results will be reported and used. Educators even disagree over how assessments should be conducted, especially when examining children who have disabilities or children who are not from the majority culture. These concerns represent only the tip of the iceberg.

You are student teaching at a time when the mere mention of National Education Goals and/or No Child Left Behind may elicit strong opinions regarding school readiness, educational performance, and program evaluation. Throughout your student teaching practicum, you will have opportunities to participate in ongoing discussions about these contemporary issues as you interact with early childhood teachers, paraprofessionals, parents, and others who share similar interests. In fact, you may even find yourself questioning what it means to expect all children to reach their highest potential or "maximal capacity" in an educational climate of high-stakes testing and accountability.

As beginning teachers, you want all children in your care to feel that their place of learning is an emotionally safe environment. Therefore, you may find yourself questioning whether or not young children should be

Voices of Reality: Student Teachers Speak

When we do assessment, they are told they are going to play a game and everyone will get a chance to play. . . . I believe the children see the timer that the teacher presses and concentrate on that rather than the task at hand. And this testing is a deciding factor of who goes to EDK [Extended Day Kindergarten].

Jackson L.

The first three days were 20-minute conferences with each student, individually, to evaluate what their ability is. We actually had students cry because they did not know the answers to some of the questions. We had to tell them each time that it is okay, that we don't expect them to know the answers; these are things that they will be able to understand at the end of kindergarten.

Nancy F.

In our multiage room, most of our first and second-graders had never seen a test like the math or reading pretests before. That, combined with some of them having a definite need to finish and be successful despite how difficult a test is, made it quite a stressful experience. Each section of the test ended in tears for at least a few. This brings up the question of whether such a test is worth it.

Saul D.

assessed at all. No matter what your reaction to the topic of assessment, this issue is not going away. Accordingly, you may want to consider how to make the process of evaluation nonstressful for children. No one wants to see children reduced to tears because they feel anxious in an unfamiliar testing situation. Therefore, the topics of assessment, testing, standards, and evaluation are important for you to consider as you prepare to enter the profession of early childhood education.

❖ ASSESSMENT: A BLESSING OR A CURSE?

A review of recent history reminds us that, in 1990, President George H. W. Bush and the nation's governors called for the establishment of National Educational Goals. The first goal was that by the year 2000, all children would be entering school ready to learn. In 1994, Congress called for the creation of "clear guidelines regarding the nature, functions, and uses of early childhood assessments" (Shepard, Kagan, & Wurtz, 1998, p. 3). Then in January of 2002, President George W. Bush signed the No Child Left Behind Act (NCLB) of 2001. The NCLB calls for the annual assessment of children in grades 3 through 8 along with the development of content and performance standards for reading, mathematics, and science. Although the regulations primarily focus on school-age children, they have an impact on the development of standards in preschool programs as well (Kagan & Scott-Little, 2004; Kendall, 2003). In fact, the federal government has instituted accountability measures that mandate biannual testing of children in Head Start programs in the areas of language, literacy, and premath. As a result, some critics decry the focus on assessment of cognitive skills rather than an emphasis on the social/behavioral development of young children (Raver & Zigler, 2004). More discussion regarding the national testing and assessment of preschoolers will no doubt continue as policymakers examine the evidence being collected over time.

What Assessment Is and What It Is Not

Assessment has been defined as "the process of documenting what children do and how they do it in order to make decisions affecting children" (Hyson, 2002, p. 62). Although definitions vary, they generally include several common ideas. For example, the process of assessment may include the following characteristics (Airasian, 2001; Mindes, 2003):

- Decision-making purpose
- Variety of methods
- Application to an individual or to a group
- Creation of one or more products that may be interpreted
- Inherent ethics and responsibilities

Assessment is so important that it is considered a right belonging to all young children. Even the youngest children deserve thoughtful "assessment that is ongoing, appropriate, and developmentally supportive" (Hyson, 2002, p. 63). It is a broad topic that includes observations, family interviews, testing, and alternative approaches to assessment, such as authentic assessment. An overview of these forms of evaluation will be discussed in this chapter as well as the appropriate uses of each in the context of early childhood education.

❖ ASSESSMENT-RELATED TERMINOLOGY

Unfortunately, some people mistake testing for assessment. This is not surprising since the media continually report test results and nationwide *test targets* as the focus of school improvement efforts. Testing, however, is not the same as assessment. Therefore, a brief overview of a few terms associated with assessment may be helpful at this point.

Several terms frequently mentioned in discussions of assessment include *testing, measurement,* and *standards.* These words are value laden in that they

High-stakes testing refers to the administration of tests the results of which are used to make important decisions affecting the future of children, teachers, schools, and educational programs.

often evoke preconceived ideas in the minds of those who hear them. This is particularly true in an educational climate in which **high-stakes testing** is commonplace (Salvia & Ysseldyke, 2004; Venn, 2004).

Testing

Testing may be defined as one form of assessment used to collect data. The data are usually reported numerically in the form of test scores. Tests are generally administered in a prescribed manner for a specific purpose. They may include many types of formal standardized tests and less formal teacher-made tests (Mindes, 2003).

When thinking about administering tests to children in early childhood programs, you should discuss several questions with your cooperating teacher and your college supervisor.

- How will this test benefit children?
- What decisions will be made as a result of the test?
- What training is necessary in order to administer the test appropriately?
- Has this test been evaluated for developmental appropriateness and linguistic appropriateness?
- How will families be informed of the test results?

Reflection on these questions will help you be prepared when families and policymakers want to know if a particular child is making progress or if a particular early childhood program is successful.

The testing of young children must proceed cautiously and responsibly (NAEYC & NAECS/SDE, 2003; Reeves, 2000). In fact, both the National Association for the Education of Young Children (NAEYC) and the Association for Childhood Education International (ACEI) urge caution regarding the standardized testing of young children. They have taken the position that no decisions should be made regarding any child based on the results of one test (Crosser, 2005).

Measurement

Measurement is a broader term than testing. It refers to "the process of determining the ability or performance level of students" (Venn, 2004, p. 5). Although a test is one kind of measurement, it is not the only kind. For example, you can collect data from the careful observation of children that will help you not only understand children's behavior but also optimize their opportunities for growth and development (Nicholson & Shipstead, 2002). Observational methods such as running records, checklists, and time sampling will be discussed later in this chapter.

Standards

Standards may be defined as shared expectations for learning and development. In other words, standards in early childhood "specify what young children should know and be able to do" (Kagan & Scott-Little, 2004, p. 390). Standards have been a fact of life in K–12 education for years; but now, with increased state investment in early childhood programs, the so-called standards movement is gaining momentum. According to a joint position statement issued by the NAEYC and the National Association of Early Childhood Specialists in State Departments of Education (NAECS/SDE), more than twenty-five states have developed standards for the education of children below kindergarten age (2002).

Care must be taken to ensure that standards are developed to benefit children rather than to harm them. For example, stimulating discussion and creating a consensus about what should be included in an early childhood program is beneficial for all. In contrast, placing negative consequences on children who do not meet prescribed standards is harmful.

NAEYC and NAECS/SDE (2002) recommend that standards contain four essential features that promote positive outcomes for children, as shown in the Figure 7.1.

The development of early childhood standards has been called "the true litmus test of the future direction of the field" (Kagan & Scott-Little, 2004, p. 395). Reaching agreement concerning appropriate standards and appropriate curricula for young children will not be easy. This is due, in part, to the fact that early childhood education is relatively unstructured in comparison with public education K–12. Consequently, you are entering the field during a significant period of transition.

This is also a period of frustration and confusion for some cooperating teachers.

Teachers with many years of experience are grappling with these issues. Assessment is truly one of education's "hot topics." When you have the opportunity, ask your colleagues for their opinions.

❖ PURPOSES OF ASSESSMENT

Four general purposes of early childhood assessment are generally acknowledged (Bowman, Donovan, & Burns, 2001; Jones, 2004; Shepard, Kagan, & Wurtz, 1998):

- To support children's learning,
- To identify those children in need of special services,

Essential Features	Characteristics
1. Developmentally appropriate content and outcomes	All domains of development and learning included
	Expectations meaningful to well-being and learning
	Expectations based on developmental research
	Expectations linked to age and/or developmental periods
	Expectations accommodate variations such as cultural, linguistic, and individual
2. Process for appropriate evaluation, review, and revision	Expectations validated through examination of effectiveness
	Wide range of participants such as families, early childhood educators, and professional groups included in examination of standards
	Information regarding standards and their implications shared openly for discussion
	Process established for ongoing examination and revision as needed to ensure continued relevancy
3. Implementation and assessment practices considered ethical and appropriate	Curriculum and its implementation promote positive learning and development
	Assessment connected to standards and yields information considered useful and valid
	Assessment information used to make decisions that benefit children
4. Support for early childhood programs, families, and professionals	Use of research findings and resources to create environments for effective implementation of standards
	Systematic, ongoing professional development for early childhood teachers and administrators
	Collaborative, cooperative approach to communicating with children's families

FIGURE 7.1   Essential Features of Beneficial Early Childhood Standards

Voice of Reality: Cooperating Teacher Speaks

I understand the importance of standards but not all "square pegs" will fit into a "round hole"—all children will never master the state standards. I tell my student teacher not to get bogged down with meeting all the standards—NO ONE has the solution to that one! Besides, don't lose those "teachable moments" because they are important also. . . . Reality is no matter what you do, some children are going to have a very hard time meeting the standards. Legislators don't have a clue—it's that simple.

Barbara L.

- To evaluate programs and to monitor trends, and
- To instill accountability.

All four of these purposes should be occurring continually (Mindes, 2003). Since young children are the central focus of everything you do, your ongoing assessment of their learning and development guides each decision you make. As you monitor the effectiveness of instructional activities, you gather information that will enable you to answer parents' questions concerning how their individual children are doing. In addition, legislators and program administrators are focusing more attention on the funding of early childhood programs. They want evidence concerning program quality and effectiveness. Assessment data also provide the information that enables you to answer their questions.

Assessment to Monitor Understanding

Assessment should benefit children. It should be related to the goals established for a particular program, and the results should be used to plan appropriate experiences for your children. You may do a *preassessment* to determine children's levels of functioning before instruction, a *formative assessment* during instruction to check progress and understanding, and then a *summative assessment* at the end of instruction to determine if your goals have been met. For example, if you are having young children follow directions to make paper bag puppets for a dramatization, you may preassess to make sure children understand the concept of what a paper bag puppet is. You may show them some sample puppets. During construction of the puppets, you may do a formative assessment to see how well children are following directions by walking around and observing progress. If you find that children are getting confused, then you will need to rephrase and/or clarify your instructions. You may need to make adaptations, such as assigning children to work with partners. Then, summative assessment of ability to follow directions will be the final product, a paper bag puppet ready for use.

Assessment as a Screening Tool

Screening is a commonly used term that refers to the process of collecting information to decide if more extensive assessment is needed. Parents of children being screened must be notified as to the purpose of the intended screening and be provided with the results of the screening. They must also be notified if further in-depth assessment is recommended. You may expect to work closely with them since they have the right to be continually involved in any decisions made regarding their children.

Children are screened at many points in their early years. For example, child care facilities, preschools, and school districts commonly conduct vision, hearing, and cognitive screening to determine which children have difficulties that warrant further testing. Screening cannot identify children as eligible to receive special services, but it can indicate which ones need in-depth evaluation (Maxwell & Clifford, 2004; Mindes, 2003; Salvia & Ysseldyke, 2004). Therefore, screening is assessment that benefits children.

You can do informal screening in your classroom in the form of a functional assessment. For example, if you are concerned that a particular child may have difficulty meeting the behavioral expectations of first grade, you can create your own rating scale to use as a referral tool.

Such an informal rating tool can at least provide you with a basis for discussion if you believe the child could benefit from behavioral support.

Assessment to Evaluate Programs and Progress

Parents and the public in general have an interest in knowing if children are making progress as a result of instruction. As a teacher, you are accountable or responsible for providing appropriate education for all the children in your care. *Accountability* is a word that is often heard these days in relation to pro-

Routine screening benefits children by locating those who have difficulties that warrant further in-depth evaluation.

Sample Informal Rating Scale

Classroom Behaviors	I (never) to 5 (always)				
Sits in circle at story time	I	2	3	4	5
Raises hand to be called on	I	2	3	4	5
Follows directions	I	2	3	4	5
Walks in line in hallway	I	2	3	4	5

(Adapted from Mindes, 2003, p. 167)

gram evaluation. Programs are often evaluated on the basis of the children's reported progress. Therefore, assessment is critical to the continuation of funding for specific programs.

This assessment can and should take many forms. For example, as a teacher, you may collect data by making observations of children. You may assemble representative samples of children's work in portfolios. You may also give tests before and after instruction based on the curriculum you are teaching. Accordingly, you can demonstrate children's progress in many ways (Rosenberg, O'Shea, & O'Shea, 1998; Salvia & Ysseldyke, 2004).

❖ FORMAL ASSESSMENT

Assessment can also be in the form of formal, standardized tests in which children's performance is compared to that of a representative sample of children of the same age or developmental level (Airasian, 2005; Sylvia & Ysseldyke, 2004).

Certainly, there are special concerns when evaluating programs based on the outcomes of tests administered to young children. Experience tells us that young children typically demonstrate extreme variability in development across domains. They also have limited ability to understand the abstract nature of testing in general. The entire concept of administering formal tests to young children has been called technically indefensible by some critics (Shepard, Kagan, & Wurtz, 1998). Nevertheless, the federal government has mandated "a new set of accountability measures that will be used to test Head Start children twice a year on language, literacy, and pre-math skills" (Raver & Zigler, 2004, p. 58). You may have the opportunity to formulate your own opinions as you observe and participate in the assessment process.

❖ INFORMAL ASSESSMENT

Informal assessments may take several forms. They should be as unobtrusive as possible so as to not interfere with children's typical behavior. Generally, use of paper and pencil is less obtrusive than use of a camera or video recorder for example.

Observation

You will find that you can learn quite a bit just from observing children and paying close attention to details. Observation is a skill that will improve with practice (Mindes, 2003). There are several techniques that you can use effectively (adapted from Daniels, Beaumont, & Doolin, 2002).

Examples of Observation Techniques

- **Event sampling:** You may wish to observe children's behavior when specific events occur. For example, you may select one or two children to observe during outside recess, particularly if you have concerns about inappropriately rough play. You may observe the kinds of social interactions that occur.
- **Time sampling:** If you wish to monitor the frequency of occurrence of particular behaviors, you may use a technique called time sampling. You observe a child for an interval of time such as 10 minutes. You have a checklist of behaviors such as "calling out" or touching others. Each time the child exhibits a behavior on the checklist, you record a tally mark on the chart. You can tailor a chart for a particular child and record on-task and off-task behaviors, for example. An advantage to this technique is that it is an objective measure of the frequency of occurrence of observable behaviors.
- **Anecdotal records:** You may use anecdotal records as a technique to record quick impressions of an event right after its occurrence. The difficulty with anecdotal records is that they are somewhat subjective. The observer can decide that a behavior is irrelevant and leave it out of the record. Nevertheless, anecdotal records can be useful in providing documentation to support a teacher's actions (Salvia & Ysseldyke, 2004).
- **Running records:** You may use running records to write a narrative of a child's behaviors to provide a sequential description of an event. Generally, a running record focuses on one child. You limit yourself to a period of time such as 15 minutes. Then you can go back over your notes and analyze evidence of particular competencies or behaviors. When two children's behaviors are described in the same narrative, the accuracy of the record declines.

Samples of various formats that may be used to collect data are included at the end of this chapter. These sample formats, adapted from Alberto and Troutman (2003), may be adjusted in many ways to meet your particular needs.

No matter which observation techniques you use, there are several tips to help you make informed decisions. Dichtelmiller (2004) recommends that you make a point of observing children daily at varying times. You can compare your notes with observations made by your cooperating teacher. When appropriate, share information with children's families in order to encourage two-way communication. For example, if you observe changes in a child's behavior, ask family members if they have noticed similar changes at home. Teacher-family partnerships benefit everyone, especially the children.

❖ AUTHENTIC ASSESSMENTS

Many advocates for young children support the use of authentic assessment as a preferred means of evaluation. Authentic assessment is an alternative to the more traditional paper-and-pencil kinds of tests. It involves activities like those commonly used in *the real world*, such as building a model, illustrating a story, performing a dramatization, or contributing to a class newspaper.

Some students are more motivated to do well on assessments if they perceive that you are asking them to do something worthwhile (Kyle & Rogien, 2004). Therefore, it makes sense to assess learners who have a wide range of interests and strengths in a variety of ways.

Children's Portfolios

Portfolios are one form of authentic assessment that provides tangible evidence of a child's progress. Many times, even young children can help select the work products to be included in their portfolios. They can attend the parent-teacher conferences and show-and-tell about each item.

The portfolio does not have to be limited to paper-and-pencil evidence of work. You can be creative about what items to place in children's portfolios. Some suggestions include the following (Gestwicki, 1999):

- Tape recording of a child speaking with you about a story as you ask questions to evaluate understanding
- Photograph of an art project
- Video recording of a dramatization
- Anecdotal records of observations
- Child's choices of "good" work

Children play an active role as they show and tell about the work chosen for inclusion in their portfolios.

You may want to collaborate with your children about what items to include in their portfolios so they feel a sense of ownership. Portfolios are most effective when they are a vehicle for active learning and the children have a "voice in the process" (Hill & Ruptic, 1994, p. 35). You can stimulate children's active involvement by encouraging them to engage in reflection.

Although portfolios represent a valuable collection of children's work, they should have a purpose, such as assessing a child's improvement over a period of time. Scoring portfolios is an issue that deserves careful attention. Scoring systems can be flawed by subjectivity so grading or scoring of portfolios has limited value (Salvia & Ysseldyke, 2004). Rubrics, rating scales, and checklists based on specific criteria need to be carefully considered. If you

---

Suggested Prompts for Reflection

- Why did you choose these pieces of work?
- What is your favorite sample of work? Why?
- What does this sample tell about you?
- What did you learn from doing this sample of work?

Format for Sample Rubric

Category	3 points	2 points	1 point
Readiness	Completely prepared and rehearsed	Somewhat prepared Rehearsal lacking	Not prepared
Stays on Topic	On topic 100%	On topic most of the time 75% or more	Hard to tell what topic was
Listens to other presentations	Listens carefully, no distracting noises	Sometimes does not appear to listen but not distracting	Sometimes does not appear to listen and makes distracting noises

choose to use portfolio assessment, then work with your cooperating teacher to develop procedures that work best for you and the children.

Performance Assessment

There may be times when you have the opportunity to use performance assessment with young children. This is assessment of behaviors that occur in simulated situations. For example, if you are teaching social skills to children who are having difficulty giving and receiving compliments, you can talk about appropriate behavior, model the desired behavior, and then set up a role-play so that children can practice giving and receiving compliments. The role-play is a contrived or simulated situation. Nevertheless, you can assess the children's behavior during this activity. In order to be effective, you should establish performance criteria before the simulation begins, explain these criteria to the children, and give feedback afterward (Rosenberg, O'Shea, & O'Shea, 1998).

❖ ALTERNATE ASSESSMENT

Ever since the passage of the Individuals with Disabilities Education Act (IDEA, 1997) and the No Child Left Behind Act (NCLB, 2001), alternative assessment has been a focus of attention. All children must be included in formal state and district assessments. Children who have severe disabilities may have an alternate assessment instead of a paper-and-pencil test. Each state may determine which children are eligible for an alternate assessment. Each state may determine what that alternate assessment will look like. You can visit the Web site for the National Center on Educational Outcomes to

Voices of Reality: Student Teachers Speak

Some teachers do the testing because they have to and others do it because they believe in results, and getting results is a way of helping a child in need ☺.

Jackson L.

Today was an early dismissal day. The afternoon was for report cards. I couldn't believe how subjective they are! Most of it is on a scale from 1 to 3, and we don't base it on grades because we don't have any! It is all backed by anecdotal records, but it is definitely subjective!

Krista U.

find out your state's current policy on alternate assessment at *http://education .umn.edu/NCEO/TopicAreas/AlternativeAssessments/StatesAltAssess.htm*. Some states require a scripted test that is video recorded. Others allow observation checklists and portfolios. Since formal assessment of young children occurs in the primary grades and now extends to four- and five-year-olds in Head Start programs, you should be aware of your state's policies regarding alternate assessment.

❖ FINAL THOUGHTS

Assessments can be challenging for all teachers, which is one reason that the purposes for assessment must be carefully considered. It is important to remember that our assessment should benefit children, not harm them. Airasian (2005) reminds us that assessment "is more than a technical activity; it is a human activity that influences and affects many people" (p. 20). As the NAEYC Code of Ethical Conduct reminds us, the special vulnerability of young children must be kept in mind as well as respect for each young child's uniqueness. Therefore, we must refrain from making hasty judgments because what we do during the important process of evaluation and assessment does indeed influence and affect many people.

ACTIVITIES FOR REFLECTION AND ACTION

1. How will you know if your children have learned as a result of your teaching?
2. Observe your cooperating teacher. What informal strategies does she use to assess student learning? What formal strategies?
3. Create a checklist that can be used to observe the behavior of a child in your class who concerns you. Use it for a brief time interval, such as 15 minutes. Share the results with your cooperating teacher.

To analyze some mini-cases and take some practice quizzes related to the content of this chapter, log on to the Companion Website at www.prenhall.com/tyminski. Go to Chapter 7 and choose from the links in the left column.

Sample Format for Event Recording ❖

Child:
Observer:
Objective: Child will demonstrate appropriate social interaction during recess.
Criterion: 100% appropriate social behavior during recess for 5 consecutive days.

Behaviors	Dates						Comments
Takes turns							
Plays with others							
Refrains from name-calling							
Refrains from physical aggression							
Total observed							

Sample Format for Time Sampling

Child:
Observer:
Objective: Child will remain on-task during seatwork.
Date:
Time Start:
Code: X = occurrence

5-Minute Interval Time Sampling

	5	10	15	20	25	30
On-task						
Verbal off-task						
Physical off-task						
Passive off-task						

Sample Format for Anecdotal Records

Child:
Others present:
Observer:
Date:
Time:
Setting:
Purpose of Observation:
Anecdote: (Include context of event, action observed, and
          conclusion of event.)

Reflection: (Include interpretation and significance of event.)

Sample Format for Running Record ❖

Child:
Observer:
Date:
Context of Observation: (Include relevant background information.)

Observation:

Reflective Comments:

CHAPTER 8

Supportive Instruction

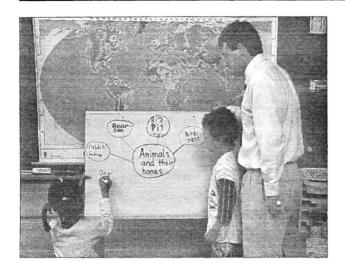

It is a general insight, which merits more attention than it receives, that teaching should not be compared to filling a bottle with water but rather to helping a flower to grow in its own way. As any good teacher knows, the methods of instruction and the range of material covered are matters of small importance as compared with the success in arousing the natural curiosity of the students and stimulating their interest in exploring on their own.

Noam Chomsky

Noam Chomsky's words are particularly relevant as you assume more and more responsibility in the planning of lessons and the implementation of developmentally appropriate curriculum. By now, you have already seen the joy and excitement young children bring to your class each day. You notice the sparkle shining in their eyes as they take pleasure in the community of mutual respect and meaningful interaction that you help create. As you begin your student teaching practicum, you may be focusing on the details of writing lesson plans that follow curriculum guides written by practicing teachers or state departments of education.

Remember that good teaching is not so much about beautifully written plans as about children. You want to nurture each child's natural curiosity and joy of learning. As you focus on your children's interests and individual needs, you will become more adept at implementing a variety of teaching strategies and integrated curriculum that engage the whole child in meaningful learning. Accordingly, you will play a significant role in helping each one of your young flowers grow.

❖ RECOGNIZING CHILDREN'S UNIQUE WAYS OF KNOWING

Research indicates that young children have unique ways of constructing meaning. As you may recall from your child development classes, young children rely heavily on sensory-motor interaction with their physical environment in order to learn. They benefit from active exploration in a social setting with other children and caring adults (Berk, 2002; Santrock, 2003; Slavin, 2003; Wilson, 2000). The challenge for you is to decide *what* to teach based on your knowledge of children's interests, experiences, and developmental levels. In addition, you must decide *how* to teach based on your knowledge of effective techniques and available technologies.

Voices of Reality: Student Teachers Speak

My first lesson on oceans—I was so nervous. I was afraid I would forget something. It wasn't until later that I realized I forgot to put the Arctic Ocean on the board. The students had no problem switching over to the fact that I was the one teaching. They participated fully—it was funny to see their reaction when tasting regular and salt water. One boy flipped because he is allergic to salt, but he calmed down when his mom said it was okay to try it. All in all it was a good day and a great lesson!

Paula M.

I taught my math lesson. When I told them to get in their groups from yesterday and do their worksheets, this is where it all went downhill—they didn't understand. I didn't know how to explain, and it was "HELL." My Egyptian girl was crying in frustration/ confusion. This made me want to cry, but I just sat with her and helped her through. Now I have to think about what went wrong and how to re-teach tomorrow.

Rosa K.

I began my moment in the spotlight by asking children to respond, by showing a "thumbs-up" sign, to the question, "Who is excited to be in school?" My query was met with a unanimous affirmative reaction. To have the opportunity to work with youngsters who have such an apparent genuine thirst for knowledge and learning, and to think that I may be an instrument in this learning, thrills me beyond description.

Karla S.

Today was a big planning day. I'm a little nervous about the things that I am being put in charge of only because I feel like I'm not being given a lot of direction. She [the teacher] told me that she will only give me limited direction because she wants to see what I come up with. . . . [I]t makes me a little uneasy. I am used to being told.

Ruth H.

As beginning teachers, you want all children to continue feeling excited to be in school. Your heart breaks as you see a child cry in frustration; your spirit lifts when you observe children making inquiries and discovering truths about their environment. As you proceed through student teaching, you will understand the meaning of supportive instruction through your own hands-on experiences. With the help of your cooperating teacher and college supervisor, you will become more confident in your ability to plan, implement, and evaluate developmentally appropriate practices in an integrated, child-centered curriculum. Then you will enable your children to experience less frustration and more joy.

❖ RELATING INSTRUCTION TO YOUNG CHILDREN'S WAYS OF KNOWING

You have likely already completed one or more courses in child development. Therefore, a repeat of basic principles is not necessary. Nevertheless, you may benefit from a brief reflection of the particular ways young children make sense of their world. After all, as Rousseau (1762/1969) wrote centuries ago, "Nature provides for the child's growth in her own fashion, and this should never be thwarted" (p. 50). Unfortunately, in misguided efforts to provide the best possible educational opportunities for young children, adults are accused of hurrying the growing-up process. According to Elkind (2001), today's child is, in fact, "the unwilling, unintended victim of overwhelming stress-the stress borne of rapid, bewildering social change and constantly rising expectations" (p. 3). Even well-intended efforts to hurry children's development may be in vain. Consider the words of the noted child development specialist, Arnold Gesell, who wrote that "enriching the child's environment and providing him with the fullest opportunities possible permits him to express himself at his very best, but it does not make him 'better' or smarter or speedier than he was born to be" (Gesell, Ilg, Ames, & Rodell, 1974, p. 15). Keep the words of these influential theorists in mind as you think about how you can create a learning environment that allows young children to maximize their biologically determined potential.

Children's Ways of Knowing

Research indicates that young children have a unique way of knowing and processing information. For example, preschool children construct meaning through direct, sensory interaction with their environment. For them, "perception conducts thought" (Wilson, 2000, p. 166). They also ask many "Why?"

questions as they try to make sense of their world. This can be frustrating and humorous at the same time as you try to give an answer and move on. For example, a four-year-old may ask to play outside and you say "Not today." She asks "Why?" You answer that it is raining hard outside. She asks "Why?" This dialogue can go on and on until you get tired or run out of answers. Your challenge may be to redirect the child to another activity and perhaps pull out a story book about a rainy day.

You may also find that your children's perceptions lead them to inaccurate interpretations of physical events (Palmer, 1995). They may even attribute human qualities to the inanimate objects in their environment such as the animal-like movement of clouds or the eyeball-like headlights of a car (Piaget, 1963; Richards & Siegler, 1986). These inaccuracies may stem from incomplete knowledge rather than from magical thinking since they disappear as children become exposed to new information over time (Woolley, 1997).

Accordingly, you may benefit from being a student of the young child's world. In other words, you observe, assist, listen intently to what children say, ask them questions, and support each child as he explores his environment and discovers his interests and strengths. Then you can make planning developmentally appropriate activities for young children a challenging opportunity to demonstrate your creativity.

As you plan opportunities for learning, keep in mind Piaget's view that children learn most effectively through active participation in their learning. In other words, they benefit from interacting with other children and with their environment (Piaget, 1971). If you want children to learn about animals, for example, take them to a zoo or an aquarium, preferably one that has a supervised "Please Touch" area for children. Your follow-up classroom activities will be more meaningful when children can relate what they have seen and experienced to what they are learning.

Scaffolding is providing a helpful structure or support for the developing child.

As you may recall from child development coursework, your active involvement in **scaffolding** children's play is strongly recommended by the work of the late developmental psychologist Lev Vygotsky. He maintained that encouragement of social interactions and make-believe activities promote children's development (Berk, 1994; Vygotsky, 1978). In fact, he said that you can help children progress toward abstract thought through make-believe play. For example, a child may begin using a toy telephone to pretend that she is talking on the phone. Later in her development, she may pick up a wooden block that represents a telephone and pretend that she is talking on the phone. You can interact with the child and show her an array of objects that can be renamed and substituted in fantasy play. For example, a carrot wrapped in a blanket becomes a baby. Follow the child's lead. You will have many opportunities to encourage communication and language acquisition as well as social skills through play.

Utilizing Children's Sensitive Periods

Young children have "sensitive periods" in which their minds are particularly receptive to learning certain types of information. They may display enthusiasm for particular activities during these periods (Humphryes, 1998; Montessori, 1967). Your recognition of these sensitive periods is critical. Once they pass, they may never return with equal intensity; and opportunities for learning may be lost (Morrison, 2000). Knowing this, you can capitalize on these sensibilities to engage them in developmentally appropriate activities related to their interests.

As an illustration, research seems to indicate that young children's brains are particularly receptive to primary language development as well as acquisition of a second language (Berk, 2002; Bredekamp & Copple, 1997). If you have children for whom English is their second language (ESL), then they need support in maintaining the language spoken at home while acquiring new language skills at school (Wong, 1992). The issues involving ESL will be discussed later in the text.

This sensitive period for language acquisition also applies to children who have special needs. For example, young children who are deaf or hearing impaired are generally able to learn American Sign Language with greater ease than their adolescent or adult counterparts (Mayberry, 1994).

In addition, young children will generally experience other sensitive periods. For example, between the ages of three and six, they may be particularly receptive to the concept of order in their environment. They may enjoy arranging tiny objects and noticing where items belong. Beginning about age six, they may experience a sensitive period characterized by a noticeable development in their imagination (Chattin-McNichols, 1992). They may enjoy so-called open-ended materials such as play dough, fabric scraps of different textures, and blocks that can have many uses. Again, the challenge for you is to create a classroom environment in which fantasy, social interactions, and hands-on exploration play a role in a child-centered, developmentally appropriate curriculum.

Applying Gardner's Theory of Multiple Intelligences

Another approach to creating a child-centered curriculum is to apply Gardner's theory of multiple intelligences (MI). This MI theory examines eight different abilities that are reflected in individuals' learning styles (Gardner, 1999). They are listed as follows:

1. *Bodily/kinesthetic:*   Ability to use one's body and to use movement to solve problems
2. *Interpersonal:*   Ability to understand and respond appropriately to other people

3. *Intrapersonal:*   Ability to understand oneself and to use that knowledge to guide behavior
4. *Linguistic:*   Ability to understand words and use language effectively
5. *Logical/mathematical:*   Ability to understand logic, patterns, and numerical reasoning.
6. *Musical:*   Ability to create rhythm and musical sounds
7. *Naturalist:*   Ability to discriminate between natural objects and understanding of the natural world
8. *Spatial:*   Ability to perceive visual-spatial relationships accurately

The implication of the MI theory is that children should be taught in a multiple ways. Therefore, as you plan instruction, you need to provide experiences in a variety of disciplines.

Since children differ in their individual strengths, you should plan lessons that involve as many of the multiple intelligences as possible. For example, if you are teaching a unit on music, you can readily incorporate a variety of activities (adapted from Driscoll & Nagel, 2005):

- Read a story about a band (linguistic intelligence).
- Collect materials from nature to use in creation of musical instruments (naturalistic, spatial, and logical/mathematical intelligence).
- Listen to a piece of music and describe the feelings it evokes (intrapersonal intelligence).
- Move to the rhythm of the music (bodily/kinesthetic intelligence).
- Work with others to form a band and put on a musical performance (interpersonal and musical intelligence).

You do not have to incorporate every one of the multiple intelligences into each lesson you teach in order to be effective. However, your children will benefit from your efforts to include experiences that utilize their diverse abilities as much as possible.

Developmentally Appropriate Practice and Curriculum

As a student of early childhood education, you have already been exposed to basic concepts of developmentally appropriate practice (DAP). These concepts have been the subject of much discussion and debate since NAEYC published position statements addressing DAP in 1986, 1987, and 1996. If you have not read NAEYC's *Developmentally Appropriate Practice in Early Childhood Programs* (Bredekamp & Copple, 1997), put this on your professional development must-read list. In fact, it would be a wise purchase to keep in your personal library as you begin your professional career. You may order it online through the NAEYC Web site at *www.naeyc.org.* As an added bonus, it is relatively inexpensive compared to many other professional resources.

Developmentally Appropriate Practice

A clarification of terms is important before discussing implementation of practices. Developmentally appropriate practice (DAP) has been characterized as "a philosophy (not a curriculum) based upon decades of developmental research and practical experience and is widely held to define best practices in the field of early childhood education" (McMullen, 1999, p. 70). It is the result of decisions teachers make based on knowledge of typical child development in all domains, knowledge of each individual child's unique needs and interests, and knowledge of the social/cultural context of the particular learning environment (Bredekamp & Copple, 1997).

If we consider DAP to be a philosophy that results in certain decisions, then we must consider guidelines supported by NAEYC as critical factors in determining best practices. According to Lerner, Lowenthal, and Egan (1998), these factors include the following:

- Integration of multiple developmental domains in the planning of children's activities
- Encouragement of children's inquiry and exploration by arranging the environment to facilitate active learning
- Progression of children's experiences from the simple and concrete to the increasingly complex and abstract
- Observation of children's individual interests and progress by a variety of means, including **authentic assessment**

> **Authentic assessment** refers to demonstration of ability to perform tasks in the context of real-life situations.

DAP versus DIP

In order to fully appreciate what developmentally appropriate practice is, we must understand what it is not. Bredecamp and Copple (1997) provide examples of appropriate practice compared with inappropriate practice for young children in the following age brackets: infants and toddlers from birth through age three, children ages three through five, and children ages six through eight. That is, developmentally inappropriate practice (DIP) may be considered the contrasted extreme of DAP or the absence of appropriate practice (Charlesworth, 1998). Figure 8.1 contains examples of DAP versus DIP for each age bracket adapted from Bredecamp & Copple (1997).

Curriculum

The term *curriculum* means different things to different people. For example, Hendrick (2003) defines curriculum as "design of experiences and activities developed by teachers to help children increase their competence" (p. 4). This definition is all inclusive and holistic; everything that happens in the child's

DAP: Infants and Toddlers	DIP: Infants and Toddlers
Adults recognize that infants have their own patterns for eating and resting so they set their own schedule.	Adults follow predictable, unchanging schedule for infant feeding and nap times.
Toddlers' environment has small defined areas for individual work/play so children don't "clump."	Toddlers' environment includes large group area for formal group activity.
DAP: Ages 3–5	**DIP: Ages 3–5**
Open classroom environment that allows for play in a variety of ways such as sand/water tables. Children given choices of activities.	Closed classroom environment with physical arrangement that primarily allows sitting and passive experiences.
DAP: Ages 6–8	**DIP: Ages 6–8**
Teachers use variety of strategies to build a sense of group as a democratic community such as regular class meetings and group decision making.	Teachers' behaviors and techniques undermine sense of community as children often work independently or in competition with others.

FIGURE 8.1 Examples of Appropriate versus Inappropriate Practice

day at the children's center, day care, or school is curriculum. Other definitions consider the curriculum to be the foundation of learning that focuses on both what and how to teach (Catron & Allen, 2003). Regardless of the definition, appropriate curriculum requires eight guidelines according to Bredekamp and Copple (1997):

- Addresses all developmental areas
- Contains relevant, engaging, and meaningful cross-disciplinary content
- Builds on prerequisite skills and knowledge
- Focuses on one subject at a time or integrates subjects to form connections
- Promotes acquisition and application of knowledge
- Encourages inquiry and active participation
- Supports family's culture and language while developing ability to participate in the shared culture and language of the general community
- Sets realistically attainable goals for developmental age and ability

With experience, you will become more and more comfortable with integrating these guidelines into your lesson planning.

❖ SUPPORTIVE INSTRUCTION IN COMMUNICATION

Because the development of communication skills is vital for the young child to interact with others and to understand the world, this area of instruction will be addressed separately. Language, literacy, and literature are three focus areas to consider when creating activities and facilitating opportunities for children to communicate their thoughts and feelings (Feeney, Christensen, & Moravcik, 2001). As a professional, you are entering into a partnership with each child's parents and family members to make decisions that affect the communication curriculum. Language skills, emergent reading and writing skills, and appreciation of literature are all areas where a home–school partnership can be an asset.

Student Teacher's Role in Language Development

As a student teacher, your role in children's acquisition of language skills is vital at all stages of child development. Research indicates that what happens to children during the first three years has a significant impact on their brain development (Shore, 1997). The implication is that, as more and more young children are receiving care in facilities other than their homes, your role as a professional early childhood caregiver becomes increasingly significant. Therefore, your use of developmentally appropriate practices in the infant and toddler years is vital. You can encourage children's language development through your interactions with them (Charlesworth, 2004; Kratcoski & Katz, 1998; Soundy & Stout, 2002).

Accordingly, during your student teaching practicum with young children, you need to create an environment that supports and encourages the sensitive periods for growth in all children. Just to show one example of how you can encourage this growth, the author will focus on language learning. Your daily conversations with children, even the youngest in your care, will encourage the development of language.

Since you have successfully completed some if not all of your child development coursework, a review of age-linked stages of language development will not be reviewed here. Instead, we will focus on what you can do to create an interactive, language–rich environment for learning. The following table gives examples of ways you can encourage the development of skills in a purposeful, social context (Beaty, 2004; Bredekamp & Copple, 1997; Catron & Allen, 2003; Dickinson & Tabors, 2002).

Supporting a Language-Rich Environment for Bilingual Children

In a joint position statement issued in 1998, the International Reading Association and the National Association for the Education of Young Children stress that our children's primary language and home culture will influence

Strategies to Encourage Language Development

1. Expand on what the child has said to make a complete thought or sentence.
   - Child says, "Puppy sad."
   - You say, "Yes, the puppy is sad."
2. Use extensions of the child's words by responding to his comments.
   - Child says, "Puppy sad."
   - You say, "The puppy is feeling sad because he wants a friend to play with."
3. Use repetitions of all or part of the child's words.
   - Child says, "Puppy sad."
   - You say, "Puppy feels sad. Time to find a friend."
4. Use self-talk of your own actions to model vocabulary and sentence structure.
   - Child says, "Puppy sad."
   - You say, "Puppy is feeling sad. Puppy is going to play with a friend."
5. Employ vertical structuring using questions to encourage conversation.
   - Child says, "Puppy sad."
   - You say, "Where is the puppy's friend?" Puppy wants to play with a friend."
6. Use fill-ins allowing the child to add words to complete statements in conversation.
   - Child says, "Puppy sad."
   - You say, "Puppy wants to go play. She feels_____."
   - Child says, "Sad!"

(Adapted from Kratcoski & Katz, 1998)

their literacy development. Furthermore, they caution us that a language and cultural *difference* is not the same as a *deficit*. Therefore, as you plan activities to promote language development, you should encourage and support bilingual children's learning of *both* languages (Catron & Allen, 2003). You can obtain storybooks in children's primary language whenever possible. For example, you can request information on good-quality books for children written in Spanish by visiting the Barahona Center Web site at *www.csusm.edu/csb*.

Creative play, field trips, and social experiences with bilingual peers and adults, for example, will provide opportunities for communication in both languages. You may wish to choose topics of study with your multicultural students and their families in mind. For example, if you study foods, families can share their unique family recipes and foods for the children to taste.

Another aspect of language development that is often overlooked is children's dialectical speech. Children may speak nonstandard English, using a dialect such as ebonics. According to Frederick Erikson (2001) and

Infancy to toddler (ages 1–3)	Repetitive jingles
	Interactive games such as pat-a-cake
	Storybook reading
	Alphabet blocks and puzzles
	Sing-a-longs
	Dramatization activities
	Predictive storybooks
	Reading poster-sized "big books"
	Exposure to literacy-rich environment
Preschool (ages 3–5)	Dramatization activities
	Predictive storybooks
	Reading big books
	Exposure to literacy-rich environment that includes books in many centers, not just library corner
	Action songs and rhymes
	Taped stories to accompany books
	Printed labels for names and objects
Kindergarten (ages 5–6)	Repeated readings of familiar stories
	Children's retelling of stories
	Teacher dictations of language experience stories
	Story reenactments and dramatic play
	Big book activities
	Games involving directions like Simon Says
	Exploration of sound-symbol relationships
	Exploration of reading and writing as a means of social communication
	Exploration of literacy rich environment
Primary grades K–3 (ages 5–8)	Daily opportunities of being read to as well as independent or teacher-supported reading
	Opportunities to communicate in writing for varied purposes
	Introduction of spelling strategies and word identification strategies
	Exposure to varied types of text in literacy rich environment
	Opportunities to collaborate in small groups

FIGURE 8.2   Activities to Encourage Literacy Development

Carlos Ovando (2001), this speech indicates differences in culture reflected in language rather than differences in social class. As a student teacher, you may model standard English, for example, but allow children to communicate "without correction or domination of conversations" (Catron & Allen, 2003, p. 228).

Antibias Curriculum

As classrooms for children of all ages are becoming more multicultural, you must be aware of the important role that curriculum can play in confronting bias. Pictures decorating your room, signs written in English and other languages, and thematic units you teach, for example, can all have a positive effect on children's acceptance of diversity. Even children as young as two or three are not too young for an antibias curricular approach as they explore human differences and similarities (Derman-Sparks & Phillips, 1997; Hendrick, 2003).

> **Antibias curriculum** refers to a model that recognizes, accepts, and respects human difference while seeking to eliminate stereotypes and bias.

In fact, toddlers may show signs of "pre-prejudices toward others based on gender or race or being differently abled" (Hunt, 1999, p. 39). Therefore, an **antibias curriculum** is an essential component of early childhood education in the twenty-first century (Henniger, 2002; Machado & Botnarescue, 2001).

According to Louise Derman-Sparks (1999), several quality markers indicate where you are on the journey to creating an effective multicultural/anti-bias program. Recommendations suggest that daily curriculum in your classroom be characterized by the following:

- Reflect children's daily life experiences, such as helping to prepare meals.
- Reflect children's cultural and individual needs with input from parents and caregivers.
- Incorporate diversity and social justice issues related to race, ethnicity, gender, disability, elders, socioeconomic status, and different definitions of family.
- Involve families, including those not fluent in English.
- Develop problem-solving strategies for resisting unfair stereotypical behaviors and improving quality of life in the community.
- Include staff representative of the community's cultural diversity.
- Engage staff in ongoing intentional reflection of personal cultural influences on behavior and attitudes.

As a student teacher, you may be expected to follow the preestablished curriculum, which may or may not include explicit, antibias elements. Even so, you may certainly incorporate many of these quality markers in your own interactions with young children.

In addition, as you plan lessons and activities, look for materials such as storybooks, toys, and prompts that are "diversity-friendly" (Hedrick, 2003;

Henniger, 2002). For example, ask yourself the following questions as you preview children's literature:

- Do the illustrations promote stereotypical behavior in regard to gender, race, ethnicity, disability?
- In the storyline, who has the power to solve problems or make decisions?
- Can you determine the perspective and/or cultural background of the author and/or the illustrator?
- Does the narrative contain loaded adjectives such as *lazy* or *primitive*? Does the author avoid the use of sexist language?

Accordingly, your choice of teaching materials can send a message to young children just as clearly as your words and behaviors.

❖ SUPPORTIVE INSTRUCTION USING AN INTEGRATED CURRICULUM

Instruction in curriculum as well as in other areas is often taught in an interdisciplinary manner rather than as individual subjects. In fact, young children's "development and learning are interconnected across and within domains" (Bredekamp & Copple, 1997, p. 98). Therefore, curriculum that is interconnected or integrated is a common-sense way to teach the whole child.

During your practicum, you may be asked to develop themes or projects that allow children to explore several disciplines at once. For example, many children's books such as *Lunch* by Denise Fleming and *Peter's Chair* by Ezra Jack Keats lend themselves to the development of children's math games (Cutler, Gilkerson, Parrott, & Browne, 2003). You may incorporate opportunities for social development, cognitive development, and fine and gross motor development as you provide hands-on opportunities for children to explore a variety of concepts. As you plan your lessons and activities for an integrated curriculum, you may wish to use a webbing process to create a visual map that shows the curricular areas represented (see Figure 8.3). In this manner, you can see where you need to add or delete items to create balance (Henniger, 2002; Krogh, 1995; Machado & Botnarescue, 2001; Workman & Anziano, 1993; Worsley, Beneke, & Helm, 2003).

Figure 8.4 provides extremely varied examples of activities that may be incorporated into an integrated curriculum (Catron & Allen, 2003; Clements & Sarama, 2003; Dodge & Colker, 2000; Feeney, Christensen, & Moravcik, 2001; Hesse & Lane, 2003; Murphy, DePasquale, & McNamara, 2003).

The integrated or balanced curriculum approach is generally considered to be responsive to children's needs and interests. It is somewhat fluid in that it "comes from the children, from their interests, activities, family

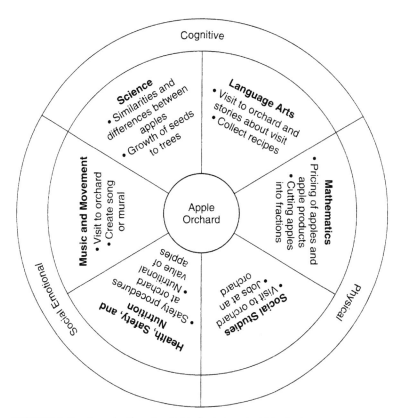

FIGURE 8.3   Sample Planning Web for Integrated Curriculum

backgrounds, and community" (Litman, Anderson, Andrican, Buria, Christy, Koski, et al., 1999, p. 5). A few curriculum models have been discussed in this chapter, but many more exist. Therefore, ongoing communication with your cooperating teacher is essential so that your planning coincides with the prevailing curricular approach used in your facility or school program.

Several generally accepted guidelines may help you as you begin planning appropriate curriculum for young children.

As you begin the planning process, listen carefully to your children. What are their questions and interests? What events are taking place in their lives? Focus on your children, and they will guide the curriculum that you plan. Also, consider what particular interests you have. Even if you must incorporate state-mandated topics into the curriculum, you can do it within the framework of children's interests, your interests, and their immediate needs (Branscombe, Castle, Dorsey, Surbeck, & Taylor, 2003; Gestwicki, 1999; Goethals & Howard, 2000; Wortham, 2002).

Study of Foods

Language Arts	Mathematics	Social Studies	Science
Storybook read-aloud	Use measuring cups and spoons to cook	Visit to grocery store	Food drying for snacks
Children's cookbook	Add ingredients	Workers who prepare foods	Seeds
Puppet drama	Sequencing in cooking activities	Use blocks to create grocery store play area	Edible plant parts (stems, fruits)
Child-authored books			
Books such as *Stone Soup* or *The Very Hungry Caterpillar*	Graph of favorite foods		Kitchen map and community map
Books with pictures by famous illustrators	Sorting food pictures by color and shape, etc.		

FIGURE 8.4 Sample of Integrated Curricular Activities

After you select a topic for your curriculum unit, then brainstorm ideas using a web. For example, if you are teaching in the fall in an area where apples are harvested, then you can easily have an apple theme as shown in Figure 8.3. You may include types of apples, taste different kinds of apples, cook foods that contain apples, create a graph of children's apple preferences, visit an apple orchard or a grocery store, create a classroom grocery store, make a book of apple recipes, read books about apples and apple products. The list can go on and on. After you complete your web, consider which activities best meet your children's needs. What skills do you want your children to develop from each activity? You can then develop your outcomes or objectives. For example, as a result of visiting an apple orchard, children will understand that workers in an orchard have different responsibilities.

The Project Approach and the Integrated Curriculum

The project approach stems from information about the use of projects in the preschools of Reggio Emilia, Italy. In the United States, early childhood teachers incorporate projects into the curriculum as an "in-depth investigation of a topic worth learning more about . . . as a research effort focused on finding answers to questions about a topic posed either by the children, the teacher, or the teacher working with the children" (Katz, 1994, p. 1). A project

Curriculum Planning Guidelines

1. Provide for multiple areas of development including cognitive, physical, emotional, linguistic, and aesthetic.
   - For example, includes materials that children can physically manipulate and enjoy.
2. Plan integrated curricular content including several disciplines.
   - For example, provide opportunities for linguistic development and social interaction.
3. Content is accessible so that children can actively participate in learning.
   - For example, conduct experiments and collect data.
4. Create opportunities for supporting children's home culture and primary language.
   - For example, use family participation and/or leadership in activities as appropriate, such as sharing cultural heritage and stories of childhood.
5. Develop realistic outcomes or goals that are attainable.
   - Provide scaffolding as needed to help children master skills such as use of scissors or access to age-appropriate computer software.
6. When using technology, integrate it into the curriculum plan and teaching process.
   - Provide for technology that enriches the learning environment such as supervised use of microscope to examine veins in leaves.

(Adapted from Gestwicki, 1999, p. 53)

is a child-centered inquiry that may incorporate activities involving multiple intelligences as well as a variety of disciplines. Project ideas often emerge from children's interests or from particular events in their lives. The projects themselves generally have three sequential phases (adapted from Driscoll & Nagel, 2005):

- **Planning phase:**   Children share information about what know and what they want to learn. They collect materials and plan experiences.
- **Activity phase:**   This phase may include field trips, guest speakers, investigation, building, reading, writing, drawing, and creating.
- **Concluding phase:**   Children demonstrate what they have learn through a variety of means such as plays, reports, stories, displays, and exhibits.

The project approach focuses on children's needs and interests as they make choices about their learning. It allows you to accommodate children with a wide range of abilities and special needs. For example, children who have attention deficit hyperactivity disorder (ADHD) often benefit from active, hands-on learning activities that allow them movement in the classroom. Children who are considered gifted may prefer to work independently or to take leadership roles in group activities. Children with cognitive impairments may benefit from working with a peer helper or a circle of friends (Choate, 2003). The project approach allows you to guide children with special needs who require assistance and to serve as a resource for others who benefit from the freedom to pursue inquiry on their own.

Content Areas and Standards

You should know that there are national and state standards for each content area such as mathematics, social studies, and science. You may be required to specify which standards you are including in each of your lesson plans. The following Web sites contain links to both national and state standards in all content areas:

> *www.educationworld.com*
> *http://edStandards.org/Standards.html*

When you check online, you will find links to national educational organizations such as the National Council of Teachers of Mathematics and the National Council of Teachers of English. Professional organizations have created national standards that are organized by grade levels. You will also find links to the standards by topic and grade level developed by each state.

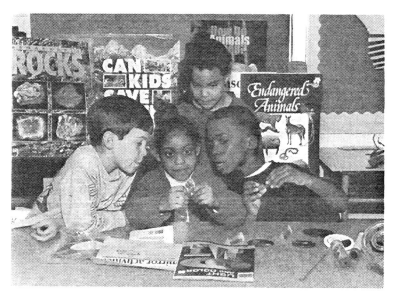

Project work provides children with opportunities to pursue their interests and make choices as they are actively engaged in learning.

In best practices, teachers integrate these content areas. As you develop lessons, note that you should also integrate content standards. Take the time to examine these standards listed in the areas of fine arts, language arts, mathematics, physical education and health, science, social science, and technology.

❖ TECHNOLOGY AND SUPPORTIVE INSTRUCTION

You can use technology effectively to support your instruction with young children. It is, however, somewhat controversial. Some critics decry technology as a potentially harmful means of denying children key developmental experiences. Others support technology as a means to extend learning opportunities. The author's opinion is that technology can be a valuable learning tool if used appropriately.

Technology in Preschool

Technology applications can be introduced in preschool and then expanded in the primary grades. Preschoolers may benefit from opportunities to explore open-ended, interactive software such as CD-ROM storybooks that allow them to have some control over the pace and content of the presentation. Children develop a sense of cause and effect as they learn that they cause animation, for example, on the screen. They may progress to developmentally appropriate software that allows them to create and illustrate their own stories (Robinson, 2003).

As a beginning teacher, you will have increasing opportunities to connect technology with your curriculum in meaningful and creative ways. In addition, you will have many decisions to make. For example, some proponents of technology discuss criteria for selecting interactive computer software for children as young as eighteen months (Robinson, 2003). Others caution against using computer technology with children younger than age three (Haughland, 1999). Some critics warn that young children's exposure to computer technology may lead to social isolation. Others report that computers lead to increased social interaction and collaboration with peers (Male, 2003; Sandholtz, Ringstaff, & Dwyer, 1997). Regardless of mixed opinions, one thing remains certain. Technology is here to stay. In 1997, the U.S. Department of Education declared children's use of technology to be a national research priority (Fischer & Gillespie, 2003; Haughland & Wright, 1997). Ultimately, you will have to make decisions based on your knowledge of each child and the technology and resources available to you.

Developmentally Appropriate Software

Certain guidelines can help you make decisions about selection of developmentally appropriate software (Dodge & Colker, 2000). For example, you may ask questions such as the following:

- Is the content free of stereotypes and bias?
- Can levels of difficulty be varied as needed?
- Can the child alter the pace of the program?
- Is the program open ended to allow for exploration?
- Is the content age appropriate?
- Does the program appeal to varying learning styles?
- Can the child operate the program independently?
- Does the program meet curricular goals and objectives?

Regardless of the software selected, you will want to engage the children in dialogue. By doing so, you will encourage them to reflect upon not only what they are doing but also why.

Assistive and Adaptive Technology

Because children with special needs are often included in early childhood programs with their typically developing peers, **assistive and adaptive technology** can be a powerful tool to encourage communication and learning. This technology is considered part of the early intervention services available under Individuals with Disabilities Education Act (IDEA) regulations, and its use is becoming more commonplace in inclusive educational settings.

During your student teaching practicum, you may have the opportunity to collaborate with early intervention special educators and support staff. You may also find yourself working closely with your cooperating teacher, families of children with special needs, and technology specialists to find tools that allow each child to take part in daily routines and activities. These tools may be high-tech devices such as electronic communication boards or low-tech devices such as weighted pencils and markers. A goal of technology is to help a child with special needs participate to the maximum extent possible in developmentally appropriate activities with same-age peers who may or may not have disabilities (Belson, 2003; Male, 2003; Mulligan, 2003). You may also assist children with special needs by doing something relatively simple such as pairing a child who has developmental delays with a typically developing child. Cooperative/collaborative learning opportunities utilizing computer software, for example, can be beneficial to both children (Dodge & Colker, 2000).

Assistive technology refers to any tool such as a switch or specialized keyboard that improves an individual's functional capabilities.

Adaptive technology refers to modifications made in traditional tools such as voice-activated software.

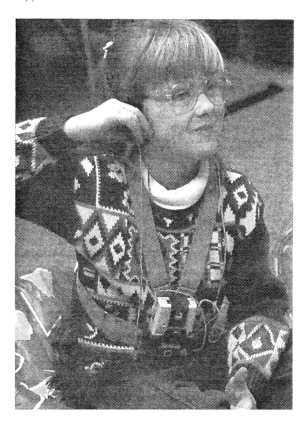

Today's inclusive classrooms often include children with special needs. Assistive technology allows children who have communication disabilities to interact with their more typically developing peers.

Voices of Reality: Student Teachers Speak

I feel that I am being an effective teacher when my students are excited about what they are learning and when they are able to make connections to other things. I know that a student is "getting" what I am teaching when they run up to me in the morning to tell me that they saw the moon (after we had talked about the moon) or when they bring in a map to show me (after we had talked about maps).

Ruth H.

I think it is harder to teach in early childhood not because of the curriculum but because of the children's needs at those ages. Anyone can stand in front of a twelfth-grade class and teach a math class. But it is a lot harder teaching a math class in the younger early childhood years.

Lauren C.

❖ FINAL THOUGHTS

Finding the right balance of supportive instruction can be a challenge as you consider children's unique ways of knowing. You plan developmentally appropriate instruction within the framework of curriculum guidelines. You are mindful of desired outcomes and accountability while providing a supportive environment for ALL children. You interconnect themes between and across domains while incorporating developmentally appropriate technology for typical children and for those with special needs. It is no wonder that these challenges can seem overwhelming at times! As you read the rest of the chapters in this text, keep in mind that you will be improving your skills in these areas throughout your professional career. Perhaps you can relate to the comments made by the student teachers in the support group.

ACTIVITIES FOR REFLECTION AND ACTION

1. Develop of list of educational materials you would include in your own classroom that promote a multicultural, antibias curriculum. Include specific examples of children's literature, toys, games, electronic media, and any other materials you deem appropriate. Reflect on why you add each item to your list.
2. Think of a topic theme that you want to teach. It may be any topic that is timely and of interesting to your children. Create a chart or a web that shows how you will integrate this theme across several disciplines.
3. Develop a plan for a thematic unit or learning centers that incorporate all of the multiple intelligences. State how each MI is incorporated into your plan.
4. Interview two teachers about the types of software they use with their students. What percentage of these programs are drill-and-practice. What creative ways can you think of to incorporate technology into your lessons?

WEBSITES

www.ecap.crc.uiuc.edu
This Web site provides access to information about the project approach.

www.childrenssoftware.com
This site provides reviews of children's computer software.

www.tamcec.org
This site is sponsored by the Council for Exceptional Children. It provides information concerning the use of assistive technology and media in the classroom.

www.dynavoxsys.com
This site provides information concerning assistive technology devices commonly used by children with special communication needs.

To analyze some mini-cases and take some practice quizzes related to the content of this chapter, log on to the Companion Website at www.prenhall.com/tyminski. Go to Chapter 8 and choose from the links in the left column.

CHAPTER 9

Understanding Diverse Communities and Interacting with Children's Families

It is that openness and awareness and innocence of sorts that I try to cultivate in my dancers. Although, as the Latin verb to educate, educere, indicates, it is not a question of putting something in but drawing it out, if it is there to begin with . . . I want all of my students and all of my dancers to be aware of the poignancy of life at that moment. I would like to feel that I had, in some way, given them the gift of themselves.

Martha Graham

As a student teacher of young children, you are in the special position of working with children who possess a refreshing sense of openness and a unique awareness of the world. Your challenge is to draw out the abilities they possess and provide them with opportunities to develop their individual potential. Giving them the gift of themselves is perhaps your greatest undertaking and your greatest joy.

This challenge is particularly notable today as the children and their families who come to you represent a greater cultural diversity than ever before in our history (Marshall, 2002). Your skill in working with culturally different children and their families is critical not only to your career as a teacher but also to the people whose lives you touch.

We cannot assume that successful completion of child development courses, teaching methodology courses, and a practicum prepares anyone for teaching in today's changing schools. Teaching competence now requires an understanding of the many social and psychological factors required to teach children from culturally diverse backgrounds. Therefore, a focused effort is necessary in order to develop their potential in a culturally responsive manner.

Voices of Reality: Student Teachers Speak

The music teacher had been teaching the kids a song that she wrote. The whole school had been reading The Quiltmaker's Gift *last week and talking about quilting. The song is about all the squares coming together to make a quilt, loving and unity. We all sang that song together. It was very moving, watching 600+ innocent kids who looked so different all singing this song about caring and togetherness. I couldn't help but tear up, and I noticed as I looked around that many of the teachers were.*

Krista U.

❖ CHANGING CULTURAL DEMOGRAPHICS

Changing demographic trends have been noticed for years as the numbers of nonwhite populations increased in the United States (Healey, 1995). In fact, predictions based on the 2000 census suggest that by the year 2020, "the relative percentages will be non-Hispanic White 64 percent, Hispanic 17 percent, African American 13 percent, and Asian 6 percent . . . and by 2020, four states—New Mexico, Hawaii, California, and Texax—and Washington, D.C., will have 'minority majority' populations" (Diller & Moule, 2005, p. 11).

Results of the 2000 census indicate that other dramatic changes are also occurring in the United States. This census attempted, for the first time, to determine the numbers of people who consider themselves to be multiracial or biracial. Accordingly, 2.4% of the nation or 6.8 million people listed themselves as multiracial. Then, 93% of this group listed themselves as biracial as follows: 32% white and another group not specified, 16% white and American Indian or Alaska Native, 13% white and Asian, and 11% white and black or African American (Grieco & Cassidy, 2001).

These changes have caused much speculation as to reasons. The increasing numbers of immigrants and changes in birthrate among some groups are generally considered to be major factors. Yearly numbers of immigrants have risen to nearly 1 million. Data from the 2000 census indicate that birthrates of whites are declining in comparison with those of Hispanic populations and Asian American populations (Diller & Moule, 2005).

Demographic Changes and Teachers

What does this dramatic increase in the nonmajority population in the United States mean for teachers? The vast majority of teachers in classrooms are still white females from middle-class family backgrounds. To make matters worse, "many Teachers of Color have been retiring, and expanding occupational options for People of Color has meant few replacements" (Diller & Moule, 2005, p. 156). If you take a look at the entering classes of colleges with teacher education programs, you will see comparatively few minorities. Speculation abounds as to the reasons, but the bottom line is that the numbers of teachers entering the professions are "becoming increasingly White" (Hodgkinson, 2002, p. 104).

Accordingly, teachers at all levels are finding that they must interact with increasingly diverse communities of children and their families. As an early childhood teacher, you can expect that you will teach children whose cultural identity is different from your own. This has definite implications for you as you consider what it means to be *culturally competent.*

Terminology

You are culturally competent, according to Diller and Moule (2005), if you have the ability to teach children from cultures that differ from yours. This requires you to have not only knowledge of other cultures but the ability to demonstrate sensitivity, awareness, and acceptance in your interactions with others. *Culture* includes identifying factors such as shared language, beliefs, values, and family traditions, to name a few. The terms *ethnic group* and *racial group* are sometimes confused. Throughout discussions in this text, the author will generally use *ethnic/racial diversity* for the purpose of convenience. However, they are not the same. An ethnic group refers to people who are distinguished from others by their cultural heritage while a racial group refers to people who are distinguished from others by their genetic heritage. It is important to note that racial identity is no longer considered purely a biological construct. It must be considered within the social context in which people construct identity (Martin & Nakayama, 2005).

Student Teaching and Becoming Culturally Competent

To interact effectively with culturally diverse children and their families, you should understand the impact that their culture has on their lives. Some researchers believe that you cannot do that effectively until you understand the impact that culture has had on your own life (Diller & Moule, 2005; Martin & Nakayama, 2005). You can begin this process of reflection by asking yourself a few questions about your own experiences.

You may want to share your responses to these questions. They can be the beginning of reflective discussions with other student teachers or with your cooperating teacher.

Questions for Cultural Reflection

1. What is your earliest memory of realizing that people differed racially or ethnically?
2. With what racial or ethnic group do you identify? When did you first realize that group had a name?
3. What is your first memory of you or anyone else being treated differently because of race or ethnicity?
4. Is there a time that you remember being especially proud of your racial or ethnic heritage?
5. Is there a time when you felt least proud of your racial or ethnic heritage?
6. How much contact have you had with racially or ethnically diverse groups of people? Has this changed over the course of your life?

(Adapted from Diller & Moule, 2005, pp. 46–47)

❖ BREAKING DOWN CULTURAL BARRIERS

Even children as young as the age of three have a superficial awareness of racial and ethnic differences (Grant & Haynes, 1995; Marshall, 2002). Children as young as kindergarten age have, in some cases, become socialized to indicate signs of racial preferences in playmates and toy selection (Diller & Moule, 2005). Therefore, you can have an important role in creating a learning climate in which diversity is not only accepted but also celebrated.

Awareness of Diversity Within Minority Cultures

As a teacher who will be communicating with children and families of various heritages, it is important to recognize the variety within the major categories of racial/ethnic groups. For example, The U.S. census category of Native American Indians and Alaska Natives includes roughly 0.9% of the population. Within that category, however, are many cultural differences. Native Americans alone include over five hundred different tribes and over three hundred reservations. About half the population lives in urban areas and half lives on reservations in rural areas throughout the United States (Diller & Moule, 2005).

Another example is the U.S. census group called Asians. They consist of roughly 3.9% of the population according to the 2000 census. Asian Americans represent at least forty-three ethnic groups consisting of twenty-eight groups in the Asian category and fifteen in the Pacific Islander category (Diller & Moule, 2005).

The point of this information is that even within a specific category, there is a significant amount of diversity between groups. Therefore, instead of accepting what the literature says about a particular racial/ethnic group, you may be better off seeking information from family members of the children in your class. If that is not possible, then information from local cultural or community centers may help you understand each culture more realistically.

Family Involvement and Cultural Diversity

The NAEYC Code of Ethical Conduct provides guidance in our dealings with all families. It tells us that we must develop positive relationships with families to ensure each child's success. Part of this obligation is to respect each family's culture, which includes its own particular language, beliefs, values, and customs. You also have an ethical obligation to involve families in all decisions regarding their children and to encourage their access to your classroom. The following questions may give you some guidelines for family involvement:

- Do you invite family members to your classroom?
- Do you consider family members to be resources?
- Do you consider families' cultural events when you plan class activities?
- Do you send home notes and class newsletters in the family's primary language?
- Do you invite extended family members to participate in your activities?
- When meetings are held to discuss plans for a child whose parent is not fluent in English, do you make sure that someone is present who can translate?

Differences in Parent-Child Communication

Since you will have open and frequent communication with families of different cultures, it may be helpful to consider differences in parent-child communication. This is important, particularly if a family's child-rearing practices are different from what you are accustomed to in your own culture. You must be careful to suspend judgment unless you have reason to believe a child's well-being is at risk.

Research indicates that there are some similarities as well as differences between cultures in child-rearing practices. Parents of all cultures tend to adapt their speech and use exaggerated intonations and simple structure when they talk to young children (Bornstein, Haynes, Pascual, Painter, & Galperin, 2002; Fernald, 1993). However, there are differences in amount of talkativeness observed. Euro-American parents and Cuban American parents have been described as extremely verbal while Native American Navajo and

Hopi parents have been described as extremely quiet with their children (Chisholm, 1989; Field & Widmayer, 1981). Therefore, the criticism has been made that programs that emphasize language use with young children do not respect the cultural diversity of language patterns in the home. This is a controversial issue with no clear-cut answer.

Similarly, cultural differences have been reported with regard to parents' responses to their children's crying as well as parents' holding practices (Trawick-Smith, 2003). Accordingly, parents may also have different ideas about how you should respond to their children based on their own cultural practice. Therefore, frequent communication is imperative to increase understanding and to build positive relationships.

❖ HOW TO DEVELOP POSITIVE HOME–SCHOOL RELATIONSHIPS

We have focused on racial/ethnic diversity of children and families you will teach as an early childhood professional. However, it is important to remember that there really is no such thing as a typical American family. It simply does not exist. Family structure has changed. Indeed the definition of what constitutes a family has changed. You are likely to have children from married couple families, blended families of married couples with children from previous relationships, single-parent families, families headed by grandparents, gay and lesbian families, and foster families. Family types are as varied and unique as the individuals they include. As you work to create positive relationships with children and their families, you have a fascinating challenge indeed!

Collaboration with Diverse Families

Understanding a particular family's unique diversity is central to developing an effective collaborative relationship with that family. It is important that you "learn from families how they define themselves within the context of observable characteristics in order to understand more clearly the attitudes and values operating within that family" (Olsen & Fuller, 1998, p. 55). You may find that your own values and ideas of what constitutes a family may be challenged. If so, then you must adapt to make your program an inviting, caring environment for each child.

Building Effective Interaction with Children's Families

Communication with families should be an ongoing process. Parent bulletin boards can be placed near your doorway so that they are easily accessible as adults drop off and pick up their children. Notices on the board should be written in more than just the majority language whenever possible. You can set aside a small section on the board for parents to bring in notices that they believe will be of interest to other parents. Even a small gesture such as placing a welcome sign written in several languages on your door sends a positive signal that all visitors are welcome.

School Visits and Interaction with Children's Families

Observe how your cooperating teacher involves families in her class activities. You will get some ideas that you want to remember when you have your own class someday. Families are often invited for special programs, but you can include them in many other ways as well. If you ask parents or extended family members to volunteer regularly, you find that they have a better understanding of what you do and what their child's day is really like. You develop a better understanding of them as well. Volunteers can also share their cultural heritage in many ways.

In addition, you can invite parents to make suggestions about ways in which they would like to contribute. When they volunteer in your room, remember to send a thank you note and acknowledge their contribution in your class newsletter.

A Culture-Friendly Room for Children and Families

The manner in which you prepare your room sends a message about how readily you celebrate diversity of all kinds. For example, your learning and activity centers should include dolls and toys that every child can relate to, such as dolls of different racial/ethnic groups and genders. The art materials, the music, and the imaginative play prompts should all reflect the children's diversity. Labels on objects around the classroom should reflect children's

---

Families Sharing Cultural Heritage

- Invite parents to share pictures, drawings, family stories, traditions, and the language of their cultural heritage.
- Encourage parents to share books and other print material or tapes that will help maintain their child's primary language.
- Have parents and children teach the class songs, dances, and crafts characteristic of their culture.
- Invite parents to participate in a school translation center, either to give or to receive assistance.
- Learn to pronounce each child's name and parent's name correctly.

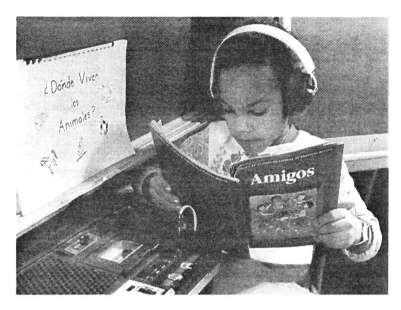

Creating a classroom climate that respects children's cultural heritage is an important goal for every early childhood professional.

home languages as well as English. Books of all types should be available that are culturally relevant and free of stereotypes. The following table provides a few examples of multicultural books recommended for young children on a variety of subjects (Valdez, 1999).

Many of these stories can be included in thematic activities related to history, cultural similarities and differences, dramatizations, language, and self-concept just to name a few.

For example, the book *Cleversticks* by B. Ashley is included in the preceding table as a choice in the category of Asian American culture. Primary-age children will enjoy listening to the story to find out what the boy is good at doing. They can follow up with a variety of activities, such as retell the story to a partner, write and/or draw what they think they do best, and make a class book or bulletin board on what our class does best. Further enrichment activities can include other storybooks about Asian American culture, foods, and use of chopsticks (Valdez, 1999).

Selection of Culturally Appropriate Books and Stories

As you are teaching the children in your practicum, you will have the opportunity to select stories or chapter books for them to enjoy. Later, when you are a professional teacher, you may be on a team to select books for a school to purchase. What guidelines will you use to choose material that is relevant and culturally appropriate? The following questions may be helpful:

Samples of Multicultural Book Choices

Topic	Books for Young Children
African American history	*On the Day I was Born*, D. Chocolate *Follow the Drinking Gourd*, J. Winter
Asian American culture	*Cleversticks*, B. Ashley *Sam and the Lucky Money*, K. Chin
Columbus—different perspectives	*A Picture Book of Christopher Columbus*, D. A. Adler *Pedro's Journal*, P. Conrad
Hispanic culture	*Poets of Puerto Rico: Don Luis Munoz Marin*, C. T. Bernier-Grand *Saturday Market*, P. Grossman
Jewish history	*A Picture Book of Anne Frank*, D. A. Adler *Matzah Ball*, M. A. Portnay
Migrant workers	*A Day's Work*, E. Bunting *Radio Man*, A. Dorros
Native American culture	*Shannon: An Ojibway Dancer*, S. King *The Gift of the Changing Women*, T. V. N. Seymour
Stereotyping and special needs	*Amazing Grace*, M. Hoffman & C. Binch *The Girl-Son*, A. E. Neuberger *My Friend Isabelle*, E. Woloson *All Kinds of Friends, Even Green!*, E. B. Senisi
Vietnamese culture	*The Lotus Seed*, S. Garland *Grandfather's Dream*, H. Keller

1. Look at the pictures in the book. Do they show people from minority cultures in non-stereotypical roles?
2. Are any references to real people or events historically accurate?
3. If there is a preface, does it make any reference to multiculturalism or cultural diversity?
4. Does the story depict people and events in an unbiased manner with regard to race, ethnicity, gender, age, and ability?

You may even be able to list additional questions that could be added to heighten awareness of cultural sensitivity. The important thing is for you to be cautious as you select materials that will influence young children's understanding of diverse people.

Home Visits and Interaction with Children's Families

Regular home visits are expected in programs such as Head Start whose clients just happen to include many people of culturally diverse heritage. Some private child care facilities and school districts encourage teachers to make home visits, but this practice is less common in these settings. If your practicum site recommends home visits, your cooperating teacher may allow you to accompany her. Generally accepted benefits of these visits include opportunities to promote home–school collaboration and opportunities to better understand the environment in which children live. However, despite your good intentions, some families may not be comfortable having you or any other teacher make a home visit; their feelings must be respected (Olsen & Fuller, 1998).

Parent Conferences and Interaction with Children's Families

During your practicum, you are likely to have the chance to observe and/or participate in parent conferences. Even though you are working to build positive relationships with families, keep in mind that some adults may be uncomfortable merely coming to their child's classroom. Although you may not feel particularly intimidating or powerful, parents still view you as being in a position of authority. Perhaps they had negative school experiences at one time; just walking into a school building may evoke unpleasant memories.

Therefore, in order for communication to be positive, you should take steps to make sure families feel comfortable in your room. Have a pleasant area for quiet conversation. Sit with them at a round table or alongside of them in chairs of equal height. This may seem simplistic, but sitting behind a desk or seating parents in children's chairs can place an emotional barrier between you and them. Engage in active listening as discussed previously in the text. Encourage sharing of information.

If the parents' primary language is not English, ask that someone be present who can translate if necessary. Also, any notes, letters, or report cards also need to be translated into the parents' primary language. Schools that have large numbers of children from homes where English is not spoken may find it helpful to contact businesses that have formed to translate regularly used documents into parents' native languages (TransAct, 2003). Many of these services are now available through Internet sites.

Cultural differences may lead to misinterpretation on your part, so be careful to remain nonjudgmental when interacting with families from cultures other than your own. For example, some parents may show up for conferences and bring the entire extended family as a show of support for their child. Others may be reluctant to show up at all because they feel that educational concerns should be left entirely up to you as the expert. You may

Frequent communication with parents builds a partnership that benefits everyone. Teachers and parents can learn from each other.

mistakenly interpret one family as being too overly protective and the other family as being too unconcerned (Parette & Petch-Hogan, 2000).

Since the parents know their child better than anyone else, this is a good opportunity for you to learn from them. A common piece of advice that you may hear is to always begin and end conferences on a positive note. If parents have many concerns, then you may want to schedule a follow-up meeting so that you and they are not rushed (Olsen & Fuller, 1998; Warner & Sower, 2005).

As previously mentioned, you are likely to be communicating with family members whose cultural heritage is different from your own; therefore a brief discussion of cultural differences in communication may be helpful.

❖ NONVERBAL CULTURAL CODES

Much has been written about differences in nonverbal communication or codes between racial/ethnic groups. The danger is that these variations can become generalized and form cultural stereotypes and prejudices. Therefore,

Voices of Reality: Student Teachers Speak

Last night was my first night of conferences. I had so much fun! I expected it to be a good night because of the conferences scheduled, and I was right. Each conference is twenty minutes. That seemed like a long time, until I sat through one. It flies! If the parents have questions or concerns (which is nice if they do!) it's rushing things. My co-op led them all but I gave my input also, and the parents seemed to value it and look at me as one of their child's teachers.

Krista U.

When I have my own conferences someday, I plan to keep little notes on each child. That way I can refer back to the personal notes and tell the parents about these. Since these would be personal, it would allow each conference to be different and break things up.

Nancy F.

One family came right before dinner time. While they were waiting they ate the entire bag of Hershey kisses we had put in a bowl in the hallway by the door. They just dropped the wrappers on the floor! Maybe that was their dinner!

Ruth H.

Being a part of parent-teacher conferences was definitely a good experience for me. As I have never been a part of conferences before. I was anxious to see how questions and comments were handled and how topics were addressed. Most of our conferences went very well and were positive. Plus, we had a good number of parents that are in the classroom helping out on a regular basis, so they are comfortable talking with my co-op and me already.

Jackson L.

There were also a handful of conferences during which the child's family issues were discussed more than their school performance. But, this was more pressing and significant to discuss at the time. It is so important to know the child from the parent's point of view.

Saul D.

we must be careful to realize that generalizations are only tentative at best. With that said, certain nonverbal behaviors or codes are often associated with particular cultural groups.

Physical Proximity, Eye Contact, and Touch

People from countries in South America and southern Europe have been described as *contact cultures* because they tend to stand close together, make frequent eye contact, and touch each other while communicating. People from countries in North America, northern Europe, and East Asia have been described as *noncontact countries* because they tend to stand further apart, make less eye contact, and touch each other less frequently while communicating (Martin & Nakayama, 2005). So, if you are a teacher whose cultural heritage is that of a noncontact country, then, in theory, you are likely to feel some discomfort when communicating with families from contact countries. These are vast generalizations. However, they indicate that we should be aware of cultural differences in behavior and be flexible with people whose cultural behaviors are different from our own.

❖ FINAL THOUGHTS

Your heightened awareness of cultural sensitivities will help you become a culturally competent teacher. This ability is no longer optional in this time of rapid demographic change. Children's families can be your best allies in learning about other cultures and incorporating them into your overall curriculum. Therefore, your sincere desire to collaborate with the families of your children will go a long way toward building the trust necessary to make that happen.

❖ ❖ ❖

ACTIVITIES FOR REFLECTION AND ACTION

1. If you have not already done so, answer the questions for cultural reflection included in this chapter (page 150).
2. Think of how you can incorporate elements of cultural diversity into a lesson(s) for children in your practicum. Develop your thoughts into a written plan.
3. How has your own racial/ethnic identity shaped your experiences as well as your attitudes toward others?
4. How does your cooperating teacher prepare for parent conferences? What have you observed that you believe contributes to effective parent-teacher conferences?
5. Add to the list of multicultural book choices suggested in this chapter. Include books and stories about all kinds of human diversity, such as people who differ by race and ethnicity and those who have special needs and abilities. You may find it helpful to write a brief description of each selection along with the reason why each is a good choice for your classroom library.

To analyze some mini-cases and take some practice quizzes related to the content of this chapter, log on to the Companion Website at www.prenhall.com/tyminski. Go to Chapter 9 and choose from the links in the left column.

CHAPTER 10

Completion of Student Teaching: Looking Ahead

You are nearing the completion of your student teaching practicum with excitement and anticipation of what lies ahead. Some of you will go on to enjoy other placements with cooperating teachers as you get closer to fulfilling the requirements of your teacher education program. For some of you, this is it . . . for now. You will be leaving your practicum site and looking ahead to graduation and the prospects of finding that professional teaching position you have wanted for so long. Others are already teaching in early childhood; but with graduation, you will have the certification status that labels you as a teacher in the profession of early childhood education. Regardless of your current status, you are approaching a transition point in your life and in the lives of the children with whom who have spent many weeks.

To teach is to touch the lives of many
and to help us learn life's lessons.
But to teach *well* is to make a difference
In all the lives you touch.

To teach is to be a parent, nurse, friend,
    and confident;
To be a supporter, a leader, and a motivator.
But to teach *well*
    is to be all of these things,
yet not lose sight of who you are.
You share a part of yourself
with all whose lives
you have touched.

To teach is to be tender,
loving, strong, an giving to all who rely
upon you;
to encourage and praise.
But to teach *well*
is to believe in what
and whom you teach.

A teacher comes to master these many jobs
throughout the years.
But those who teach *well*
Recognize that there
Will always be more
To learn in life's journey,
And they never hesitate
To strive to learn it.

Donna Bulgar

Donna Bulgar's words are worthwhile to keep in mind as you approach this transition. You know that you will be a lifelong learner. You will always strive to improve your teaching and keep up with new information in a field that is never stagnant. The challenge for you then is not to teach, but to teach *well*.

Voices of Reality: Student Teachers Speak

Well, I just want you to know that my full time in the classroom went very well, and I feel prepared and ready to set out and find my own classroom! ☺ After my week was done, it is now twice as hard to give the subjects back to my co-op. I am getting more sad as each day passes. I can't believe it is time to do my last calendar until I have my own classroom.

Jackson L.

I have started doing observations in other classrooms. The teachers I've been to so far have apologized for not having something more exciting for me to observe but it really doesn't matter. I love just sitting there and looking around the room, how it's set up, bulletin boards, etc. You can learn so much just from that! It's also interesting to see different teachers' styles, which usually come out no matter what they're doing at the time. This isn't an opportunity I'll have again. Real teachers can't just leave their classroom to spy on their friends, so I want to take full advantage of this while I can!

Krista U.

The time is drawing near for you to leave your practicum site. You need to consider how that transition should occur.

❖ LEAVING YOUR STUDENT TEACHING PRACTICUM

As your final official day in your student teaching practicum approaches, you may be feeling a well-deserved sense of satisfaction. You have worked hard and learned more than you probably realize right now. You have formed relationships with your cooperating teacher and other colleagues in the building. Perhaps, even more important, you have formed relationships with young children and their families. How you leave is as important as how you began.

Leaving Your Cooperating Teacher and Colleagues

A sincere note of thanks is appropriate. The author's personal preference is a hand-written note rather than a computer-generated one. The extra time it takes for you to write a note by hand is appreciated. It is neither necessary nor expected for you to buy a gift for your cooperating teacher. If you have formed collegial relationships with co-workers, administration, support staff, and volunteers, you should make of point of visiting them to say your good-byes during your last week of placement. You never know when you may be working with these people once again during your career, and you want to leave on the best possible terms.

Leaving the Children in Your Placement

Leaving the children is another issue altogether. You should prepare the children for your departure well in advance. They may have questions about why you are leaving and why you cannot stay with them. Some children who have formed attachments with you may cry at the thought of your leaving. If it is realistic that you can return to visit them after your last day of placement, then telling them about your return visit will help make the adjustment easier.

Although not required, some student teachers make a simple, inexpensive gift for each of their children. For example, a card with a picture taken of you and each child makes a special remembrance. Some student teachers choose to give a gift to the whole class. It does not have to be anything expensive. It could be a plant for the classroom that everyone can enjoy or a new fish for the class aquarium. In some practicum settings, it is customary for the cooperating teacher and the children to have a going-away party for the student teacher who is leaving. This is certainly not a universal practice, but it happens frequently. It is somewhat of a ritual that signifies endings and new beginnings.

Saying good-bye is an important part of bringing closure to your student teaching experience. Children may not understand why you have to leave, so this can be a difficult transition for them and for you.

Final Evaluation of Student Teaching Practicum

Some teacher education programs require a meeting at the end of the practicum among you, your cooperating teacher, and your college supervisor in order to evaluate your performance. At the very least, you will receive written evaluations at the end of the semester from your cooperating teacher noting your strengths and areas of needed improvement. The evaluation forms vary from state to state and, to some degree, from college to college. Grading requirements also vary; some programs assign a pass/no pass while others assign letter grades to student teaching.

If this is your final practicum before graduation, there will be forms submitted by your college certification officer according to your state's procedures for certification. Your college supervisor is often the person who makes sure that all paperwork is in order and ready for the certification officer to process immediately following graduation.

In addition, some colleges routinely give each student teacher the opportunity to evaluate her cooperating teacher and, in some cases, her college supervisor. If this is the case in your program, you may have the opportunity to recommend that a particular cooperating teacher be used again as a role model for student teachers—or not. You may comment on the helpfulness and frequency of suggestions you received for improvement.

You may also have an opportunity to do a self-evaluation at the end of your experience. Some colleges require self-evaluation in the form of an exit portfolio presentation. Others require a written self-analysis to present to your college supervisor.

These questions will begin to prepare you for the kinds of questions you will be asked in job interviews.

Suggestions for Postpracticum Reflection

- How have you grown as a person as a result of your practicum experience? As a teacher?
- What do you want other people to know about your teaching?
- If you have a portfolio, what does it reveal about you as a teacher?
- How are you a different person as a result of your practicum experience?
- What do you see as your strengths as a teacher? Your areas of needed improvement?
- What evidence can you provide that indicates your skill level in the competencies required by your program?

❖ PLANNING AHEAD AFTER GRADUATION

A few weeks after graduation, you will receive your teacher certificate. However, many early childhood centers and school districts will go ahead and offer you a contract as a certified early childhood teacher with oral or written verification from your college that you have met criteria for certification and your paperwork is being processed. Unless you already have a position, you need to think about the job application/interview process before graduation day.

Networking

Think about where you would like to teach. You may be limited to certain areas because of family obligations or other concerns. Perhaps you want to take a risk and move to a completely new area. These are all decisions you must consider. How do you decide what to do?

Networking or talking with people in your field of study is one option. Teachers at your practicum site may also have information about positions that will be available in the near future. In addition, most colleges have career and counseling centers that are helpful. They usually keep a file of your resume, letters of recommendation, and transcripts for prospective employers. They also notify students when job recruiters are coming on campus and serve as a good resource of information about job opportunities in various locations (Goethals & Howard, 2000; Pelletier, 2004).

Resume Writing

If you are uncertain about how to write an effective resume and cover letter, then check with your career and counseling center. They may have helpful software programs on their computers that you can use free of charge. They may offer workshops on resume writing and interview skills.

You can also find helpful information about resume writing by going online. Suggestions include the following:

- *www.resume.monster.com*
- *www.studentcenter.com*
- *www.careerlab.com*
- *www.1.umn.edu/ohr/ecep/resume/*

These sites include hints about writing good resumes as well as databases of resumes for varied purposes that you may examine (Goethals & Howard, 2000). Even when you have your resume written, ask someone such as one of your professors or an advisor to read it over. Objective feedback is always helpful. A sample resume is included at the end of the chapter to give you some ideas about format and content.

Job Fairs

Your teacher education program and your career and counseling center will receive notices about job fairs being held in your area. Independent child development centers, religiously affiliated schools, and international schools rarely participate in these events. These are usually attended by representatives from public school districts. They often have administration and teachers in attendance who are looking for people in specific areas such as early childhood education or special education.

The fairs are usually held in a location that is convenient to a number of teacher education programs. School districts from near and far will set up tables from which to hand out literature about their districts, their geographic area, and applications. If you arrive at the fair early, before the lines get long, you can often get an interview on the spot. Even if you are not sure where you want to teach, this is a good chance to learn about opportunities you had not even considered.

When you attend a job fair, be sure to take multiple copies of your resume with you and dress professionally. Some students prepare packets that include a resume, copies of recommendation letters, and copies of Praxis test scores to hand out to districts of particular interest. Since you may have the opportunity to be interviewed, you want to wear the same type of attire you would wear to a more formal interview. Therefore, leave the casual jeans and sneakers at home. Your college supervisor or your career and counseling center can give you guidance about appropriate interview clothing in your area if you are unsure what to wear.

Applications

Some states now use a common application form for all teaching positions in the public school districts. You can go to the Department of Education Web site for your state and find out if that is the case in your location. Rather than contact each individual district, you can download the common application and duplicate it for all districts. If you prefer private schools or child development centers, you will have to write each facility individually. You can even locate available positions in early childhood education by going online at *www.early.childhood.teacher.jobs.monster.com.*

When you send an application, always include a cover letter in which you give a brief introduction and indicate why you are applying to that facility. You can personalize your cover letter by sending it to a specific administrator. Your teacher education department and/or your career and counseling

Suggestions for Effective Cover Letters

- Personalize your letter to a particular person who is involved in hiring rather than a generic "To whom it may concern."
- Limit your letter to one page.
- Check to make sure your spelling and grammar are absolutely perfect. Have someone else proofread your letter also.
- Use your permanent address rather than a temporary school address.
- If you heard about the position in the newspaper or somewhere else, state that. If you are merely exploring the possibility that a position may be available in the near future, state that.
- State why you think this school, center, or district is a good match for you.
- State your qualifications, such as graduation date with degree and/or certification in early childhood education.
- Request an interview. Mention your enclosed resume and the portfolio you will have available at the interview.
- Close with a polite thank you.

(Adapted from Pelletier, 2004)

center can help you obtain the names of the appropriate people who should receive your application. A good cover letter can get your application the attention it deserves.

A sample cover letter is included at the end of the chapter.

❖ INTERVIEWS

When your college's career and counseling center announces that recruiters are coming to campus for interviews, check the list carefully. Some recruiters may specify early childhood positions. Others may just say elementary education. You can interview with either. Remember, the elementary education recruiter may have positions available in a range of grades, including K–3.

Even if you are not particularly interested in the programs or the districts represented by certain recruiters, you should go and have the interview anyway. The more experience you have with the interview process, the more relaxed and better you will do in the interviews you really care about.

Preparation for the Interview

If the campus career and counseling center offers a workshop, you may benefit from hearing their interview tips. Also, ask your college instructors, other students, and teachers you know for sample interview questions to think about. Then practice role-playing the interview and your answers to various questions.

When you have an interview scheduled, do a little background preparation. For example, check to see if the program or district has an internet site. If it does, then read the information carefully. It may reveal interesting information, such as the program's philosophy, mission, curriculum, student population, and demographics. You will make a better impression at the interview if you are informed.

If you have the opportunity, ask ahead of time who will be conducting the interview. You do not want to go in expecting to be interviewed by one person and then find out when you get there that five administrators from various buildings will all be interviewing you at the same time. If you know what to expect, you will be less nervous.

Make sure that you know what interview clothing you plan to wear so that you do not have to be concerned about your appearance.

Sample Interview Questions

Every interview will be somewhat unique because of the nature of the particular program and the people who are doing the hiring. It is common practice, however, for schools to conduct screening interviews either in person or over the phone. These interviews may be relatively brief, even twenty or thirty minutes. Some schools then call a few people back for a second interview or to teach a demonstration lesson.

Interviews generally begin with a few minutes of small talk to make you relax a little before the interview gets under way. A number of questions seem to keep turning up on interviews frequently enough that a few of them are listed here for you to think about.

Some of these questions refer to topics you may have discussed throughout your teacher education program, such as your philosophy of education

Voices of Reality: Student Teachers Speak ❖

The only thing I was missing was a pin to put on my jacket. The afternoon before my first interview, I spent an hour at the mall looking for a shiny pin that went with my suit jacket. I finally found one I liked. I knew if they asked me a question I didn't know the answer to, they might be distracted by my pin. That way they might not see the look on my face. *I figured I would have time to come up with something to say and I know it sounds crazy but it worked! Oh well, go figure.*

Jasmine L.

Frequently Asked Interview Questions

1. Why did you decide to apply for this position?
2. What is your philosophy of teaching?
3. Why did you decide to become a teacher?
4. How do other people describe you?
5. What are the qualities of a good teacher?
6. Why should we hire you?
7. What does your classroom look like?
8. What is your greatest strength? Greatest weakness?
9. What procedures do you use for discipline?
10. How would you handle an angry parent?
11. Where do you see yourself in five years?
12. Do you have any questions you would like to ask us?

and the qualities of a good teacher. Other questions may surprise you. They are intended to catch you off guard. For example, the question asking you to name your greatest weakness is a trick question. You should answer carefully by turning your so-called weakness into a strength. You might comment, "I tend to think about my work when I am at home, and I spend much of my free time planning activities for my class. I know I really should work on balancing my time a little better." This response makes you sound like someone who is really dedicated to being a good teacher. On the other hand, if you say that "my weakness is that I tend to procrastinate," then your weakness sounds like a weakness. Therefore, when in doubt, take your time, pause, think a moment, and then answer a question. You will appear to be giving careful consideration to your answers.

In spite of your best preparation, you may be asked questions you did not expect. Perhaps you will be asked questions you thought were really good ones. Several student teachers have been collecting some of their favorite interview questions.

Additional Interview Tips

Have a couple of questions in mind that you can ask the interviewers. Do not ask what the starting salary is, even if you really want to know. Instead, ask questions that will cause the interviewer to think. For example, you might ask what opportunities for professional growth they offer their teachers. What is their philosophy regarding inclusion? What changes do they foresee for their school or district in the next five years?

Voices of Reality: Student Teachers Speak

I took a few minutes to collect some of my BEST and WORST interview questions:

Best Questions

1. **In one minute, sell yourself.**   I was shocked when I heard this question because I honestly never thought I'd hear this one. This question allowed me to highlight those qualities that I have that would set me apart from someone else.

2. **How do you know when a child has been successful?**   It also demonstrates to the interviewer how this teacher perceives himself in the classroom. Whether success is determined from what the students have achieved or what the teacher has done.

3. **Do you know a good listener? Describe them to me.**   MY FAVORITE QUESTION BY FAR! (because I really liked my answer too ☺)

   Listening requires one to go beyond listening to the words that come from that child's mouth. It's about allowing the person to talk and "figure" things out for themselves before one would even consider offering any advice.

4. **What do you think a child's definition of FAIR is?**   I liked this because I never thought about it being asked in an interview. It's something to ponder. What is your definition of FAIR? But more importantly, working with children, what is their definition of FAIR?

Worst Questions

1. **What is your weakness?**   It's about rephrasing the question. Don't say this is my weakness. I remember what I said, I said, I don't know whether or not this is my fault, but if you're looking for something that I lack, I don't have professional experience.

2. **What's your position on assessment?**   This question was very tough. I had to take a side without being wishy washy and explain why I thought exactly what I did.

3. **What types of assessment methods have you used?**   This was also extremely difficult. I talked about what I thought would be best and what I would attempt to use in my classroom such as portfolios and rubrics.

Destiny M.

Try to keep in mind a few general guidelines for nonverbal communication during your interview. For example, make eye contact, refrain from crossing your arms or your legs, keep your jacket unbuttoned and your hands out of your pockets. Try not to "talk with your hands" but leave them open and relaxed. These tips will help you send the nonverbal signals that you are a confident, cooperative, and open person (Fuller & Olsen, 1998).

Try to relax and enjoy the interview process. Remember that you are also deciding if the position available is a "good fit" for you.

Follow-Up to your Interview

After your interview is over, reflect on your experience. If possible, write down as many of your interview questions as you can remember. Each time you go through this process, you will become more confident and self-assured.

Within the next day or two, send a thank-you note. You can call the school secretary to verify the names and correct spellings of the people who interviewed you. The school will contact you concerning the next steps; either a second interview or a demonstration lesson are common practices. If you hear nothing or if you receive a rejection letter, then move on and prepare for your next interview. You may have several interviews in a row and then be in the fortunate position of having more than one offer. In that case, do not feel pressured to sign a contract quickly. It is all right to say that you need to think it over because you have another offer pending.

❖ FINAL THOUGHTS

As you complete your student teaching practicum, you will have many decisions to make. It is an exciting period of your life. If you do not already have a job, the process of finding a professional teaching position can be

Voices of Reality: Student Teachers Speak

In another couple of months I will be looking for a job! ☺ I am wondering and concerned how the children will do when I am not here. I did not know if that is something I should think about, but I do . . . I am really going to miss these kids!! One mom said "I pray to God every night for teachers like you." I was so amazed and flattered. More and more I can teach kindergarten. and I will be determined to get a job in this class/age level ☺.

Jasmine L.

Sample Format for Cover Letter

Permanent Address
City, State
April 25, 2005

Dr. Jane Doe
Superintendent
Good School District
City, State

Dear Dr. Doe:
I am applying for the early childhood teaching position that is posted on the Good School District Web page. I will be graduating from Good College this May with certification in Early Childhood Education.

Your school district has an excellent reputation for its strong instructional programs designed for a diverse population of students. My course of study included field experiences in multicultural settings with children of mixed abilities. and I have experience working collaboratively with others. I believe my background would be a good fit for your district.

Enclosed please find my resume. I will be available at your convenience for an interview. I look forward to meeting you. Thank you for your consideration.

Sincerely,
Grade A. Applicant

Sample Format for Resume

GRADE A. APPLICANT
Permanent Address
City, State
phone:
e-mail:

OBJECTIVE	**Teacher: Early Childhood Education**
EDUCATION	**Good College** City, State Degree—Date Major:
STUDENT TEACHING	**Early Childhood Center** **Pre-K Teacher** City, State Dates

Responsibilities:
* (Briefly list activities as bulleted items.)
*
*
*

Local School District
Grade 2 Teacher
City, State
Dates

Responsibilities:
*
*
*
*

RELATED ACTIVITIES	Counselor, Good Summer Camp, Dates Volunteer Tutor, After School Program, Dates Art Instructor, Good Community Center, Dates
CREDENTIALS	Good College Career Planning Center City, State Phone:

nerve wracking as well as rewarding. Keep in mind that you have many re-sources at your disposal to help you, and do not hesitate to ask for assis-tance. The time will come before you know it when you will be a mentor for others who follow the path you have chosen. This is indeed a lifelong jour-ney: to teach *well* and to learn life's lessons as you make a difference in the lives you touch.

ACTIVITIES FOR REFLECTION AND ACTION

1. How will you leave the children in your practicum? What will you do for a good-bye activity?
2. Review the interview questions in this chapter. Plan how you would answer each question.

To analyze some mini-cases and take some practice quizzes related to the content of this chapter, log on to the Companion Website at www.prenhall.com/tyminski. Go to Chapter 10 and choose from the links in the left column.

Code of Ethical Conduct

❖ PREAMBLE

NAEYC recognizes that many daily decisions required of those who work with young children are of a moral and ethical nature. The NAEYC Code of Ethical Conduct offers guidelines for responsible behavior and sets forth a common basis for resolving the principal ethical dilemmas encountered in early childhood care and education. The primary focus is on daily practice with children and their families in programs for children from birth through 8 years of age, such as infant/toddler programs, preschools, child care centers, family child care homes, kindergartens, and primary classrooms. Many of the provisions also apply to specialists who do not work directly with children, including program administrators, parent and vocational educators, college professors, and child care licensing specialists.

❖ CORE VALUES

Standards of ethical behavior in early childhood care and education are based on commitment to core values that are deeply rooted in the history of our field. We have committed ourselves to

- Appreciating childhood as a unique and valuable stage of the human life cycle
- Basing our work with children on knowledge of child development
- Appreciating and supporting the close ties between the child and family
- Recognizing that children are best understood and supported in the context of family, culture, community, and society
- Respecting the dignity, worth, and uniqueness of each individual (child, family member, and colleague)
- Helping children and adults achieve their full potential in the context of relationships that are based on trust, respect, and positive regard

❖ CONCEPTUAL FRAMEWORK

The Code sets forth a conception of our professional responsibilities in four sections, each addressing an arena of professional relationships: (1) children, (2) families, (3) colleagues, and (4) community and society. Each section includes an introduction to the primary responsibilities of the early childhood practitioner in that arena, a set of ideals pointing in the direction of exemplary professional practice, and a set of principles defining practices that are required, prohibited, and permitted.

The ideals reflect the aspirations of practitioners. **The principles** are intended to guide conduct and assist practitioners in resolving ethical dilemmas encountered in the field. There is not necessarily a corresponding principle for each ideal. Both ideals and principles are intended to direct practitioners to those questions which, when responsibly answered, will provide the basis for conscientious decisionmaking. While the Code provides specific direction and suggestions for addressing some ethical dilemmas, many others will require the practitioner to combine the guidance of the Code with sound professional judgment.

The ideals and principles in this Code present a shared conception of professional responsibility that affirms our commitment to the core values of our field. The Code publicly acknowledges the responsibilities that we in the field have assumed and in so doing supports ethical behavior in our work. Practitioners who face ethical dilemmas are urged to seek guidance in the applicable parts of this Code and in the spirit that informs the whole.

Ethical Dilemmas Always Exist

Often, "the right answer"—the best ethical course of action to take is not obvious. There may be no readily apparent, positive way to handle a situation. One important value may contradict another. When we are caught "on the horns of a dilemma," it is our professional responsibility to consult with all relevant parties in seeking the most ethical course of action to take.

❖ SECTION I: ETHICAL RESPONSIBILITIES TO CHILDREN

Childhood is a unique and valuable stage in the life cycle. Our paramount responsibility is to provide safe, healthy, nurturing, and responsive settings for children. We are committed to support children's development, respect individual differences, help children learn to live and work cooperatively, and promote health, self-awareness, competence, self-worth, and resiliency.

Ideals

I-1.1.   To be familiar with the knowledge base of early childhood care and education and to keep current through continuing education and in-service training.

I-1.2.   To base program practices upon current knowledge in the field of child development and related disciplines and upon particular knowledge of each child.

I-1.3.   To recognize and respect the uniqueness and the potential of each child.

I-1.4.   To appreciate the special vulnerability of children.

I-1.5.   To create and maintain safe and healthy settings that foster children's social, emotional, intellectual, and physical development and that respect their dignity and their contributions.

I-1.6.   To support the right of each child to play and learn in inclusive early childhood programs to the fullest extent consistent with the best interests of all involved. As with adults who are disabled in the larger community, children with disabilities are ideally served in the same settings in which they would participate if they did not have a disability.

I-1.7.   To ensure that children with disabilities have access to appropriate and convenient support services and to advocate for the resources necessary to provide the most appropriate settings for all children.

Principles

P-1.1.   Above all, we shall not harm children. We shall not participate in practices that are disrespectful, degrading, dangerous, exploitative, intimidating, emotionally damaging, or physically harmful to children. This principle has precedence over all others in this Code.

P-1.2.   We shall not participate in practices that discriminate against children by denying benefits, giving special advantages, or excluding them from programs or activities on the basis of their race, ethnicity, religion, sex, national origin, language, ability, or the status, behavior, or beliefs of their parents. (This principle does not apply to programs that have a lawful mandate to provide services to a particular population of children.)

P-1.3.   We shall involve all of those with relevant knowledge (including staff and parents) in decisions concerning a child.

P-1.4.   For every child we shall implement adaptations in teaching strategies, learning environment, and curricula, consult with the family, and seek recommendations from appropriate specialists to maximize the potential of the child to benefit from the program. If, after these efforts have been made to work with a child and family, the child does not appear to be benefiting from a program, or the child is seriously jeopardizing the ability of other children to benefit from the program, we shall communicate with the family and appropriate specialists to determine the child's current needs; identify the setting and services most suited to meeting these needs; and assist the family in placing the child in an appropriate setting.

P-1.5. We shall be familiar with the symptoms of child abuse, including physical, sexual, verbal, and emotional abuse, and neglect. We shall know and follow state laws and community procedures that protect children against abuse and neglect.

P-1.6. When we have reasonable cause to suspect child abuse or neglect, we shall report it to the appropriate community agency and follow up to ensure that appropriate action has been taken. When appropriate, parents or guardians will be informed that the referral has been made.

P-1.7. When another person tells us of a suspicion that a child is being abused or neglected, we shall assist that person in taking appropriate action to protect the child.

P-1.8. When a child protective agency fails to provide adequate protection for abused or neglected children, we acknowledge a collective ethical responsibility to work toward improvement of these services.

P-1.9. When we become aware of a practice or situation that endangers the health or safety of children, but has not been previously known to do so, we have an ethical responsibility to inform those who can remedy the situation and who can protect children from similar danger.

❖ SECTION II: ETHICAL RESPONSIBILITIES TO FAMILIES

Families are of primary importance in children's development. (The term family may include others, besides parents, who are responsibly involved with the child.) Because the family and the early childhood practitioner have a common interest in the child's welfare, we acknowledge a primary responsibility to bring about collaboration between the home and school in ways that enhance the child's development.

Ideals

I-2.1. To develop relationships of mutual trust with families we serve.

I-2.2. To acknowledge and build upon strengths and competencies as we support families in their task of nurturing children.

I-2.3. To respect the dignity of each family and its culture, language, customs, and beliefs.

I-2.4.   To respect families' childrearing values and their right to make decisions for their children.

I-2.5.   To interpret each child's progress to parents within the framework of a developmental perspective and to help families understand and appreciate the value of developmentally appropriate early childhood practices.

I-2.6.   To help family members improve their understanding of their children and to enhance their skills as parents.

I-2.7.   To participate in building support networks for families by providing them with opportunities to interact with program staff, other families, community resources, and professional services.

Principles

P-2.1.   We shall not deny family members access to their child's classroom or program setting.

P-2.2.   We shall inform families of program philosophy, policies, and personnel qualifications, and explain why we teach as we do. Which should be in accordance with our ethical responsibilities to children (see Section I).

P-2.3.   We shall inform families of and when appropriate, involve them in policy decisions.

P-2.4.   We shall involve families in significant decisions affecting their child.

P-2.5.   We shall inform the family of accidents involving their child, of risks such as exposures to contagious disease that may result in infection, and of occurrences that might result in emotional stress.

P-2.6.   To improve the quality of early childhood care and education, we shall cooperate with qualified child development researchers. Families shall be fully informed of any proposed research projects involving their children and shall have the opportunity to give or withhold consent without penalty. We shall not permit or participate in research that could in any way hinder the education, development, or well-being of children.

P-2.7.   We shall not engage in or support exploitation of families. We shall not use our relationship with a family for private advantage or personal gain, or enter into relationships with family members that might impair our effectiveness in working with children.

P-2.8.   We shall develop written policies for the protection of confidentiality and the disclosure of children's records. These policy documents shall be made available to all program personnel and families. Disclosure of children's records beyond family members, program personnel, and consultants having an obligation of confidentiality shall require familial consent (except in cases of abuse or neglect).

P-2.9. We shall maintain confidentiality and shall respect the family's right to privacy, refraining from disclosure of confidential information and intrusion into family life. However, when we have reason to believe that a child's welfare is at risk, it is permissible to share confidential information with agencies and individuals who may be able to intervene in the child's interest.

P-2.10. In cases where family members are in conflict, we shall work openly, sharing our observations of the child, to help all parties involved make informed decisions. We shall refrain from becoming an advocate for one party.

P-2.11. We shall be familiar with and appropriately use community resources and professional services that support families. After a referral has been made, we shall follow up to ensure that services have been appropriately provided.

❖ SECTION III. ETHICAL RESPONSIBILITIES TO COLLEAGUES

In a caring, cooperative work place, human dignity is respected, professional satisfaction is promoted, and positive relationships are modeled. Based upon our core values, our primary responsibility in this arena is to establish and maintain settings and relationships that support productive work and meet professional needs. The same ideals that apply to children are inherent in our responsibilities to adults.

A. Responsibilities to Co-Workers

Ideals

I-3A.1. To establish and maintain relationships of respect, trust, and cooperation with co-workers.

I-3A.2. To share resources and information with co-workers.

I-3A.3. To support co-workers in meeting their professional needs and in their professional development.

P-3A.4. To accord co-workers due recognition of professional achievement.

Principles

P-3A.1. When we have concern about the professional behavior of a co-worker, we shall first let that person know of our concern, in a way that shows respect for personal dignity and for the diversity to be found among staff members, and then attempt to resolve the matter collegially.

P-3A.2   We shall exercise care in expressing views regarding the personal attributes or professional conduct of co-workers. Statements should be based on firsthand knowledge and relevant to the interests of children and programs.

B. Responsibilities to employers

Ideals

I-3B.1.   To assist the program in providing the highest quality of service.
I-3B.2.   To do nothing that diminishes the reputation of the program in which we work unless it is violating laws and regulations designed to protect children or the provisions of this Code.

Principles

P-3B.1.   When we do not agree with program policies, we shall first attempt to effect change through constructive action within the organization.
P-3B.2.   We shall speak or act on behalf of an organization only when authorized. We shall take care to acknowledge when we are speaking for the organization and when we are expressing a personal judgment.
P-3B.3.   We shall not violate laws or regulations designed to protect children and shall take appropriate action consistent with this Code when aware of such violations.

C. Responsibilities to employees

Ideals

I-3C.1.   To promote policies and working conditions that foster mutual respect, competence, well-being, and positive self-esteem in staff members.
I-3C.2.   To create a climate of trust and candor that will enable staff to speak and act in the best interests of children, families, and the field of early childhood care and education.
I-3C.3.   To strive to secure equitable compensation (salary and benefits) for those who work with or on behalf of young children.

Principles

P-3C.1.   In decisions concerning children and programs, we shall appropriately utilize the education, training, experience, and expertise of staff members.

P-3C.2. We shall provide staff members with safe and supportive working conditions that permit them to carry out their responsibilities, timely and nonthreatening evaluation procedures, written grievance procedures, constructive feedback, and opportunities for continuing professional development and advancement.

P-3C.3. We shall develop and maintain comprehensive written personnel policies that define program standards and, when applicable, that specify the extent to which employees are accountable for their conduct outside the work place. These policies shall be given to new staff members and shall be available for review by all staff members.

P-3C.4. Employees who do not meet program standards shall be informed of areas of concern and, when possible, assisted in improving their performance.

P-3C.5. Employees who are dismissed shall be informed of the reasons for their termination. When a dismissal is for cause, justification must be based on evidence of inadequate or inappropriate behavior that is accurately documented, current, and available for the employee to review.

P-3C.6. In making evaluations and recommendations, judgments shall be based on fact and relevant to the interests of children and programs.

P-3C.7. Hiring and promotion shall be based solely on a person's record of accomplishment and ability to carry out the responsibilities of the position.

P-3C.8. In hiring, promotion, and provision of training, we shall not participate in any form of discrimination based on race, ethnicity, religion, gender, national origin, culture, disability, age, or sexual preference. We shall be familiar with and observe laws and regulations that pertain to employment discrimination.

❖ SECTION IV: ETHICAL RESPONSIBILITIES TO COMMUNITY AND SOCIETY

Early childhood programs operate within a context of an immediate community made up of families and other institutions concerned with children's welfare. Our responsibilities to the community are to provide programs that meet its needs, to cooperate with agencies and professions that share responsibility for children, and to develop needed programs that are not currently available. Because the larger society has a measure of responsibility for the welfare and protection of children, and because of our specialized expertise in child development, we acknowledge an obligation to serve as a voice for children everywhere.

Ideals

I.4.1. To provide the community with high-quality (age and individually appropriate, and culturally and socially sensitive) education/care programs and services.

I-4.2. To promote cooperation among agencies and interdisciplinary collaboration among professions concerned with the welfare of young children, their families, and their teachers.

I-4.3. To work, through education, research, and advocacy, toward an environmentally safe world in which all children receive adequate health care, food, and shelter, are nurtured, and live free from violence.

I-4.4. To work, through education, research, and advocacy, toward a society in which all young children have access to high-quality education/care programs.

I-4.5. To promote knowledge and understanding of young children and their needs. To work toward greater social acknowledgment of children's rights and greater social acceptance of responsibility for their well-being.

I-4.6. To support policies and laws that promote the well-being of children and families, and to oppose those that impair their well-being. To participate in developing policies and laws that are needed, and to cooperate with other individuals and groups in these efforts.

I-4.7. To further the professional development of the field of early childhood care and education and to strengthen its commitment to realizing its core values as reflected in this Code.

Principles

P-4.1. We shall communicate openly and truthfully about the nature and extent of services that we provide.

P-4.2. We shall not accept or continue to work in positions for which we are personally unsuited or professionally unqualified. We shall not offer services that we do not have the competence, qualifications, or resources to provide.

P-4.3. We shall be objective and accurate in reporting the knowledge upon which we base our program practices.

P-4.4. We shall cooperate with other professionals who work with children and their families.

P-4.5. We shall not hire or recommend for employment any person whose competence, qualifications, or character makes him or her unsuited for the position.

P-4.6. We shall report the unethical or incompetent behavior of a colleague to a supervisor when informal resolution is not effective.

P-4.7. We shall be familiar with laws and regulations that serve to protect the children in our programs.

P-4.8. We shall not participate in practices which are in violation of laws and regulations that protect the children in our programs.

P-4.9. When we have evidence that an early childhood program is violating laws or regulations protecting children, we shall report it to persons responsible for the program. If compliance is not accomplished within a reasonable time, we will report the violation to appropriate authorities who can be expected to remedy the situation.

P-4.10. When we have evidence that an agency or a professional charged with providing services to children, families, or teachers is failing to meet its obligations, we acknowledge a collective ethical responsibility to report the problem to appropriate authorities or to the public.

P-4.11. When a program violates or requires its employees to violate this Code, it is permissible, after fair assessment of the evidence, to disclose the identity of that program.

❖ STATEMENT OF COMMITMENT

As an individual who works with young children, I commit myself to furthering the values of early childhood education as they are reflected in the NAEYC Code of Ethical Conduct.

To the best of my ability I will

- Ensure that programs for young children are based on current knowledge of child development and early childhood education.
- Respect and support families in their task of nurturing children.
- Respect colleagues in early childhood education and support them in maintaining the NAEYC Code of Ethical Conduct.
- Serve as an advocate for children, their families, and their teachers in community and society.
- Maintain high standards of professional conduct.
- Recognize how personal values, opinions, and biases can affect professional judgment.
- Be open to new ideas and be willing to learn from the suggestions of others.
- Continue to learn, grow, and contribute as a professional.
- Honor the ideals and principles of the NAEYC Code of Ethical Conduct.

Adams, N. G., Shea, C. M., Liston, D. D., & Deever, B. (1998). *Learning to teach: A critical approach to field experiences.* Mahwah, NJ: Lawrence Erlbaum Associates.

Airasian, P. W. (2001). *Classroom assessment concepts and applications* (4th ed.). Boston: McGraw-Hill.

Airasian, P. W. (2005). *Classroom assessment: Concepts and applications* (5th ed.). Boston: McGraw-Hill.

Alberto, P. A., & Troutman, A. C. (2003). *Applied behavior analysis for teachers.* Upper Saddle River, NJ: Merrill/ Prentice Hall.

Alger, H. A. (1984). Transitions: Alternatives to manipulative management techniques. *Young Children, 39*(5), 16–26.

Allen, K., Henke, L., Harris, F., Baer, D., & Reynolds, N. (1967). The control of hyperactivity by social reinforcement of attending behavior in a preschool child. *Journal of Educational Psychology, 58,* 231–237.

Allen, K. E., & Schwartz, I. S. (2001). *The exceptional child. Inclusion in early childhood education.* Clifton Park, NY: Thomas Delmar Learning.

Anderson, N. A. (1998). Providing feedback to preservice teachers of reading in the field. *Reading Research and Instruction, 37,* 123–136.

Anderson, N. A., & Radencich, M. C. (2001). The value of feedback in an early field experience: Peer, teacher, and supervisor coaching. *Action in Teacher Education, 23*(3), 66–74.

Aronson, E., Wilson, T. D., & Akert, R. M. (2002). *Social psychology* (4th ed.). Upper Saddle River, NJ: Merrill/ Prentice Hall.

Armentrout, W. D. (1927). *The conduct of student teaching in teachers colleges.* Greeley: Colorado State Teachers College.

Barnett, W. S. (1998). Long-term effects on cognitive development and school success. In W. S. Barnett & S. S. Boocock (Eds.), *Early care and education for children in poverty: Promises, programs, and long-term results* (pp. 11–44). Albany, NY: SUNY Press.

Barnett, W. S., & Hustedt, J. T. (2003). Preschool: The most Important grade. *Educational Leadership, 60*(7), 54–57.

Barnett, W. S., & Camilli, G. (2002). Conpensatory preschool education, cognitive development and

"race." In J. M. Fish (Ed.), *Race and intelligence: Separating science from myth* (pp. 369–406). Mahwah, NJ: Erlbaum.

Baruth, L. G., & Manning, M. L. (2003). *Multicultural counseling and psychotherapy. A lifespan perspective.* Upper Saddle River, NJ: Merrill/Prentice Hall.

Beaty, J. J. (2002). *Observing development of the young child* (5th ed.). Upper Saddle River, NJ: Merrill/Prentice Hall.

Beaty, J. J. (2004). *Skills for preschool teachers* (7th ed.). Upper Saddle River, NJ: Merrill/Prentice Hall.

Belson, S. I. (2003). *Technology for exceptional learners.* Boston: Houghton Mifflin.

Benesh, B., Arbuckle, M., Robbins, P., & D'Arcangelo, M. (1998). *Facilitator's guide. The brain and learning.* Alexandria, VA: ASCD.

Bergan, J. R., (1977). *Behavioral consultation.* Upper Saddle River, NJ: Merrill/Prentice Hall.

Berk, L. E. (1976). How well do classroom practices reflect teacher goals? *Young Children, 32*(1), 64–81.

Berk, L. E. (1994). Vygotsky's theory: The importance of make-believe play. *Young Children, 50*(1), 30–39.

Berk, L. E. (2002). *Infants and childhood* (4th ed). Boston: Allyn & Bacon.

Bernat, V. (1993). Teaching peace. *Young Children, 48*(3), 36–39.

Betz, C. (1994). Beyond time-out: Tips from a teacher. *Young Children, 49*(3), 10–14.

Bey, T. M., & Holmes, C. T. (1992). *Mentoring: Contemporary principles.* Reston, VA: Association of Teacher Educators.

Birchak, B., Connor, C., Crawford, K. M., Kahn, L. H., Kaser, S., & Short, K. (1998). *Teacher study groups: Building community through dialogue and reflection.* Urbana, IL: National Council of English Teachers.

Blair, T. R., & Jones, D. L. (1998). *Preparing for student teaching in a pluralistic classroom.* Needham Heights, MA: Allyn & Bacon.

Blue, T. W., Boothby, P. R., O'Grady, R. J., Toro, J. A., & Tyminski, C. R. (1999, winter). Good things take time (Unless you get a little help from your friends). *AILCTE Views and News, 10*(4).

Blue, T. W., Boothby, P. R., Newell, E. A., O'Grady, R. J., & Tyminski, C. R. (2001). *Student Teacher Evaluation*

Summary. (Available from Elizabethtown College, Department of Education, Elizabethtown, PA 17022).

Boreen, J., Johnson, M. K., Niday, D., & Potts, J. (2000). *Mentoring beginning teachers: Guiding, reflecting, coaching.* York, ME: Stenhouse Publishers.

Bornstein, M. H., Haynes, O. M., Pascual, L., Painter, K. M., & Galperin, D. (2002). Play in two societies: Persuasiveness of process, specificity of structure. In Paludi, M. A. (Ed.), *Human development in multicultural contexts.* Upper Saddle River, NJ: Merrill/Prentice Hall.

Bourdieu, P. (1984). *Distinction: A social critique of the judgment of taste* (R. Nice, trans.). Cambridge, MA: Harvard University Press.

Bowers, C. A., & Flinders, D. J. (1990). *Responsive teaching: An ecological approach to classroom practices of language, culture, and thought.* New York: Teachers College Press.

Bowman, B. T., Donovan, M. S., & Burns, M. S. (Eds.). (2001). *Eager to learn. Educating our preschoolers.* Washington, DC: National Academy Press.

Branscombe, N. A., Castle, K., Dorsey, A. G., Surbeck, E., & Taylor, J. B. (2003). *Early childhood curriculum. A constructivist perspective.* Boston: Houghton Mifflin.

Brazelton, T. B., & Sparrow, J. D. (2001). *Touchpoints three to six.* Cambridge, MA: Perseus Publishing.

Bredekamp, S. (Ed.). (1987). *Developmentally appropriate practice in early childhood programs serving children from birth through age 8.* Washington, DC: National Association for the Education of Young Children.

Bredekamp, S., & Copple, C. (Eds.). (1997). *Developmentally appropriate practice in early childhood programs* (rev. ed.). Washington, DC: National Association for the Education of Young Children.

Bredekamp, S., & Willer, B. (1993). Professionalizing the field of early childhood education: Pros and cons. *Young Children, 48*(3), 82–84.

Brewer, J. (2001). *Introduction to early childhood education preschool through primary grades* (4th ed.). Boston: Allyn & Bacon.

Brice, A. E. (2002). *The hispanic child.* Boston: Allyn & Bacon.

Brill, N. I., & Levine, J. (2002). *Working with people* (7th ed.). Boston: Allyn & Bacon.

Brookfield, S. D. (1990). *The skillful teacher.* San Francisco: Jossey-Bass.

Brophy, J. (1988). Educating teachers about managing classrooms and students. *Teaching and Teacher Education, 4*(1), 1–18.

Brophy-Herb, H. E., Kostelnik, M. J., & Stein, L. C. (2001). A developmental approach to teaching about ethics using the NAEYC code of ethical conduct. *Young Children, 56*(1), 80–84.

Bruneau-Balderrama, O. (1997). Inclusion: Making it work for teachers, too. *The Clearing House, 70*(6), 328–330.

Buttery, T. J., & Weller, L. D. (1988). Group clinical supervision: A paradigm for preservice instructional enhancement. *Action in Teacher Education, 10*, 61–73.

Cadwell, L. B. (2003). *Bringing learning to life. The Reggio approach to early childhood education.* New York: Teachers College Press.

Campbell, D. M., Melenyzer, B. J., Nettles, D. H., & Wyman, R. M. (2000). *Porfolio and performance assessment in teacher education.* Boston: Allyn & Bacon.

Canter, L. (1976). *Assertive discipline: A take-charge approach for today's educator.* Seal Beach, CA: Canter & Associates.

Canter, L., & Canter, M. (1992). *Lee Canter's assertive discipline. Positive behavior management for today's classroom.* Santa Monica, CA: Lee Canter & Associates.

Carter, C. W. (1998). The use of journals to promote reflection. *The Journal of the Association of Teacher Educators, 19*(4), 39–42.

Carter, R. T. (1990). Cultural value differences between African Americans and White Americans. *Journal of College Student Development, 31*, 72.

Caruso, J., & Fawcett, M. T. (1986). *Supervision in early childhood education.* New York: Teachers College Press.

Caspi, A. (1998). Personality development across the life course. In N. Eisenberg (Ed.), *Handbook of child psychology: Vol.3. Social, emotional, and personality development* (5th ed.) (pp. 311–388). New York: Wiley.

Catron, C. E., & Allen, J. (2003). *Early childhood curriculum* (3rd ed.). Upper Saddle River, NJ: Merrill/Prentice Hall.

Charles, C. M. (1996). *Building classroom discipline.* White Plains, NJ: Longman.

Charles, C. M. (2002). *Essential elements of effective discipline.* Boston: Allyn & Bacon.

Charlesworth, R. (2000). Developmentally appropriate practice is for everyone. In M. A. Jensen & M. A. Hannibal (Eds.), *Issues, advocacy, and leadership in early education* (2nd ed.) (pp. 170–175). Boston: Allyn & Bacon. (Reprinted from *Childhood Education, 74*, 274–283, 1998, Association for Childhood Education International).

Charlesworth, R. (1998). Developmentally appropriate practice is for everyone. *Childhood Education; 74*(5): 274–283.

Charlesworth, R. (2004). *Understanding child development* (4th Ed.). Albany, NY: Delmar.

Chattin-McNichols, J. (1992). *The Montessori controversy.* Albany, NY: Delmar.

Children's Defense Fund. (2002, June). *The state of children in America's union: A 2002 action guide to leave no child behind (PDP: 2268K). Washington, DC.*

Chisholm, J. S. (1989). Biology, culture, and the development of temperament: A Navajo example. In J. K. Nugent, B. M. Lester, & T. B. Brazelton (Eds.), *Biology, culture, and development* (pp. 341–364). Norwood, NJ: Ablex.

Choate, J. S. (Ed.). (2003). *Successful inclusive teaching. Proven ways to detect and correct special needs* (4th ed.). Boston: Allyn & Bacon.

Clements, D. H., & Sarama, J. (2003). Young children and technology. What does research say? *Young Children, 58*(6), 34–40.

Clewett, A. S. (1988). Guidance and discipline: Teaching young children appropriate behavior. *Young Children, 43*(3), 26–31.

Cole, A. L., & Knowles, J. G. (2000). *Researching teaching. Exploring teacher development through reflexive inquiry.* Boston: Allyn & Bacon.

Cole, A. L., & Knowles, J. G. (2000). *Researching Teaching. Exploring teacher development through reflexive inquiry.* Boston: Allyn & Bacon.

Condin, K. A., & Tobin, T. J. (2001). Using electronic and other new ways to help students improve their behavior. Functional behavioral assessment at work. *Teaching Exceptional Children, 34*(1), 44–51.

Copeland, W. D., & Jamgochian, R. (1985). Colleague training and peer review. *Journal of Teacher Education, 36*(2), 18–21.

Covey, S. R. (1992). *Principle-centered leadership.* New York: Fireside.

Crosser, S. (2005). *What do we know about early childhood education?* Clifton Park, NY: Thomson Delmar Learning.

Cruickshank, D. R., Jenkins, D. B., Metcalf, K. K. (2003). *The act of teaching* (3rd ed.). Boston: McGraw-Hill.

Cutler, K. M., Gilkerson, D. Parrott, S., & Browne, M. T. (2003). Developing math games based on children's literature. *Young Children; 58*(1): 22–27.

D'Arcangelo, M. (2000). The scientist in the crib. A conversation with Andrew Meltzoff. *Educational Leadership; 58*(3): 8–13.

Daniels, D. H., Beaumont, L. J., & Doolin, C. A. (2002). *Understanding children. An interview and observation guide for educators.* Boston: McGraw-Hill.

Danielson, C. (1996). *Enhancing professional practice: A framework for teaching.* Alexandria, VA: Association for Supervision and Curriculum Development.

Davis, M. D., Kilgo, J. L., & Garnel-McCormick, M. (1998). *Young children with special needs: A developmentally appropriate approach.* Boston: Allyn & Bacon.

DeBord, K., Hestenes, L. L., Moore, R. C., Cosco, N., & McGinnis, J. R. (2002). Paying attention to the outdoor environment is as important as preparing the indoor environment. *Young Children, 57*(3), 32–34.

Derman-Sparks, L. (1999). Markers of multicultural/antibias education. *Young Children, 54*(5), 43.

Derman-Sparks, L., & Phillips, C. B. (1997). *Teaching/Learning antiracism: A developmental approach.* New York: Teachers College Press.

DeVries, R., & Zan, B. (1995). Creating a constructivist classroom atmosphere. *Young Children, 51*(1), 4–13.

Dewey, J. (1933). *How we think.* Chicago: Henry Regnery.

Dewey, J. (1959). The child and the curriculum. In M. Dworkin (Ed.), *Dewey on education.* New York: Teachers College Press. (Original work published 1902)

Dichtelmiller, M. L. (2004). Experiences from the field. New insights into infant/toddler assessment. *Young Children, 59*(1), 30–33.

Dickinson, D. K., & Tabors, P. O. (2002). Fostering language and literacy in classrooms and homes. *Young Children, 57*(2), 10–18.

Dieker, L. A., & Barnett, C. A. (1996). Effective co-teaching. *Teaching Exceptional Children, 29*(1), 5–7.

Dietz, M. E. (1995). Using portfolios as a framework for professional development. *Journal of Staff Development, 16*(2), 40–43.

Diller, J. V., & Moule, J. (2005). *Cultural competence. A primer for educators.* Belmont, CA: Thomson Wadsworth.

Dodge, D. T., & Colker, L. J. (2000). *The creative curriculum* (3rd ed.). Washington, DC: Teaching Strategies, Inc.

Dreikurs, R., & Grey, L. (1968). *Logical consequences: A new approach to discipline.* Reprinted 1993. New York: Plume.

Driscoll, A., & Nagel, N. G. (2005). *Early childhood education, birth–8. The world of children, families, and educators* (3rd ed.). Boston: Allyn & Bacon.

Ducette, J. P., Sewell, T. E., & Shapiro, J. P. (1996). Diversity in education : Problems and possibilities. In F. B. Murray (Ed.), *The teacher educator's handbook* (pp. 323–380). San Franciso: Jossey-Bass Publishers.

Duckworth, S., Smith-Rex, S., Okey, S., Brookshire, M. A., Rawlinson, D., Rawlinson, R., et al. (2001).

Wraparound services for young schoolchildren with emotional and behavioral disorders. *Teaching Exceptional Children, 33*(4), 54–60.

Dufour, R. (2002). The learning centered principal. *Educational Leadership, 59*(8) 12–15.

Duke, D. L. (1987). Environmental influences. In M. J. Dunkin (Ed.), *The international encyclopedia of teaching and teacher education* (pp. 548–553). New York: Pergamon.

Eaton, D. E. (2002). Family child care accreditation and professional development. *Young Children, 57*(1), 23.

Egan, G. (2002). *The skilled helper.* (7th ed.). Pacific Grove, CA: Brooks/Cole Publishing.

Eisner, E. W. (2002). The kind of schools we need. *Phi Delta Kappan, 83*(8), 576–583.

Elkind, D. (2001). *The hurried child* (3rd ed.). Cambridge, MA: Perseus Publishing.

Elster, C. A. (1994). "I guess they do listen": Young children's emergent readings after adult read-alouds. *Young Children, 49*(3), 27–31.

Erikson, F. (2001). Culture in society and in educational practices. In Banks, J. A., & Banks, C. A. (Eds.), *Multicultural education: Issues and perspectives* (4th ed.) (pp.31–58). New York: John Wiley and Sons.

Executive summary. (2002). *In early-childhood education and care: Quality counts, 21*(7), 8–9.

Faber, A., & Mazlish, E. (1982). *How to talk so kids will listen and listen so kids will talk.* New York: Avon.

Fantuzzo, J. W., Davis, G. Y., & Ginsburg, M. D. (1995). Effects of parent involvement in isolation or in combination with peer tutoring on student self-concept and mathematics achievement. *Journal of Educational Psychology; 87*:272–281.

Feeney, S., Christensen, D., & Moravcik, E. (2001). *Who am I in the lives of children?* (6th ed.). Columbus, OH: Merrill/Prentice Hall.

Feitler, F., & Tokar, E. (1992). Getting a handle on teacher stress: How bad is the problem? *Educational Leadership, 49*(6), 456–458.

Fernald, A. (1993). Approval and disapproval: Infant responsiveness to vocal affect in familiar and unfamiliar languages. *Child Development, 64*, 657–674.

Field, T. M., & Widmayer. S.M. (1981). Mother-infant interactions among lower SES black, Cuban, Puerto Rican, and South American immigrants. In T. M. Field, A. M. Sostek, P. Vietze, & P. H. Leiderman (Eds.), *Culture and early interactions* (pp. 41–60). Hillsdale, NJ: Erlbaum.

Fields, M.V., & Boesser, C. (2002). *Constructive guidance and discipline* (3rd ed.). Upper Saddle River, NJ: Merrill/Prentice Hall.

Fischer, M. A., & Gillespie, C. W. (2003). Computers and young children's development. *Young Children, 58*(4), 85–91.

Flicker, E. S., & Hoffman, J. A. (2002). Developmental discipline in the early childhood classroom. *Young Children, 57*(5), 82–89.

Flynn, L. L., & Kieff, J. (2002). Including everyone in outdoor play. *Young Children, 57*(3), 20–26.

Foster, M. (1994). Educating for competence in community and culture: Exploring the views of exemplary African-American teachers. In M. J. Shujaa (Ed.), *Too much schooling, too little education: A paradox of black life in white societies* (pp. 221–244). Trenton, NJ: African World Press.

Freeman, N. K. (2000). Professional ethics: A cornerstone of teachers' preservice curriculum. *Action in Teacher Education, 23*(3), 12–18.

Freidus, H. (1996). Mentoring portfolio development. In N. Lyons (Ed.), *With portfolio in hand: Validating the new teacher professionalism* (pp. 51–68). New York: Teachers College Press.

Fromberg, D. P. (1997). The professional and social status of the early childhood educator. In J. P. Isenberg & M. R. Jalongo (Eds.), *Major trends and issues in early childhood education* (pp. 188–204). New York: Teachers College Press.

Fuller, F. F., & Brown, O. H. (1975). Becoming a teacher. In K. Ryan (Ed.), *Teacher Education.* (Seventy-fourth Yearbook of the National Society for the Study of Education). Chicago: University of Chicago Press.

Fuller, M. L. (1976). Multicultural concerns and classroom management. In C. A. Grant & M. L. Gomez (Eds.), *Making schooling multicultural* (pp. 133–158). Upper Saddle River, NJ: Prentice Hall.

Fuller, M. L. (2001). Multicultural concerns and classroom management. In C. A. Grant & M. L. Gomez (Eds.), *Campus and classroom. Making schooling multicultural* (2nd ed., pp. 109–134), Upper Saddle River, NJ: Merrill/Prentice Hall.

Fuller, M. L., & Olsen, G. (1998). *Home-school relation. Working successfully with parents & families.* Boston: Allyn & Bacon.

Gardner, H. (1999). *Intelligence reframed: Multiple intelligences for the 21st century.* New York: Basic Books.

Gartrell, D. (1995). Misbehavior or mistaken behavior? *Young Children, 50*(5), 27–34.

Gartrell, D. J. (1998). *A guidance approach for the encouraging classroom.* Albany, NY: Delmar/Thomson.

Gartrell, D. (2002). Replacing time-out. Part two—using guidance to maintain an encouraging classroom. *Young Children, 57*(2), 36–43.

Gellman, E. S. (1992–1993). The use of portfolios in assessing teacher competence: Measurement issues. *Action in Teacher Education, 14*(4), 39–44.

Genishi, C. (2002). Young English language learners. *Young Children, 57*(4), 66–72.

Gesell, A., Ilg, F., Ames, L.B., & Rodell, J. (1974). *Infant and child in the culture of today* (rev. ed.). New York: Harper & Row.

Gestwicki, C. (1999). *Developmentally appropriate practice* (2nd ed.) Boston: Delmar Publishers.

Glasser, W. (1989). *The quality school. Managing students without coercion.* New York: HarperCollins Publishers.

Glasser, W. A. (1988). *Choice theory in the classroom.* New York: Harper Collins Publishing.

Glasser, W. A. (1988). *Choice theory.* A new psychology of personal freedom. New York: Harper Collins Publishing.

Glasser, W. A. (1965). *Reality therapy.* New York: Harper Collins Publishing.

Glasser, W. A. (1969). *Schools without failure.* New York: Harper Collins Publishing.

Glasser, W. A. (1986). *Control theory in the classroom.* New York: Harper Collins Publishing.

Glasser, W. A. (1988). *Choice theory in the classroom.* New York: Harper Collins Publishing.

Glickman, C. (1981). *Developmental supervision: Alternative practices for helping teachers improve instruction.* Alexandria, VA: Association for Supervision and Curriculum Development.

Goethals, M. S., & Howard, R. A. (2000). *Student teaching. A process approach to reflective practice.* Upper Saddle River, NJ: Merrill/Prentice Hall.

Goodman, Y. (1998). Kid watching: An alternative to testing. *National Elementary Principal, 57*(4), 41–45.

Gordon, T. (1974). *Teacher effectiveness training.* New York: Wyden.

Governor's Commission on Early Learning. (2000). *Early learning birth to age five.* Seattle, WA: Author.

Grant, C. A., & Gomez, M. L. (2001). *Campus and classroom* (2nd. Ed.). Upper Saddle River, NJ: Prentice Hall.

Grant, D., & Haynes, D. (1995). A developmental framework for cultural competence training with children. *Social Work in Education, 17,* 171–182.

Greenbaum, P. E., & Greenbaum, S. D. (1983). Cultural differences, nonverbal regulation, and classroom interaction: Sociolinguistic interference in American Indian Education. *Peabody Journal of Education, 61*(1), 16–33.

Greenberg, P. (Ed.). (1999). Using NAEYC's code of ethics to negotiate professional problems. *Young Children, 54*(6), 56–57.

Grieco, E. M., & Cassidy, R. C. (2001). *Overview of race and Hispanic origin, 2000.* Washington, DC: U.S. Department of Commerce, Economics and Statistics Administration, U.S. Census Bureau.

Guyton, E., & McIntyre, D. J. (1990). Student teaching and school experiences. In W. R. Houston (Ed.), *Handbook of research on teacher education* (pp. 514–534). New York: Macmillan Publishing Co.

Hale, J. (1994). *Unbank the fire.* Baltimore: Johns Hopkins University Press.

Hall, E. T. (1977). *Beyond culture.* Garden City, NJ: Anchor Press.

Hamner, T. J., & Turner, P. H. (1996). *Parenting in contemporary society* (3rd ed.). Boston: Allyn & Bacon.

Hatch, D. D. (1993). Early encounters: Coaching in teacher education. In R. H. Anderson, K. J. Snyder, & J. M. Bahner (Eds.), *Clinical supervision: Coaching for higher performance* (pp. 169–182). Lancaster, PA: Technomic.

Haughland, S. W. (1999). What role should technology play in young children's learning? *Young Children, 54*(6), 6–31.

Haughland, S. W., & Wright, J. L. (1997). *Young children and technology: A world of discovery.* Boston: Allyn & Bacon.

Healey, J. F. (1995). *Race, ethnicity, gender, and class: The sociology of group conflict and change.* Thousand Oaks, CA: Pine Forge Press.

Hendrick, J. (2003). *Total learning. Developmental curriculum for the young child* (6th ed.). Upper Saddle River, NJ: Merrill/Prentice Hall.

Henniger, M. L. (2002). *Teaching young children: An introduction* (2nd ed.). Upper Saddle River, NJ: Merrill/Prentice Hall.

Henry, M. A., Beasley, W. W., & Brighton, K. L. (2002). *Supervising student teachers the professional way* (6th ed.). Terre Haute, IN: Sycamore Press.

Hesse, P., & Lane, F. (2003). Media literacy starts young. An integrated curriculum approach. *Young Children, 58*(6), 20–26.

Hiemstra, R., & Sisco, B. (1990). *Individualizing instruction.* San Francisco: Jossey-Bass.

Hill, B. C., & Ruptic, C. (1994). *Practical aspects of authentic assessment: Putting the pieces together.* Norwood, MA: Christopher-Gordon Publishers.

Hilliard, A. (1999). Toward better teacher education: A conversation with Asa Hilliard. *Educational Leadership, 56*(8), 58–62.

Hodgkinson, H. (2002). Demographics and teacher education. *Journal of Teacher Education, 53*(2), 102–105.

Hole, S., & McEntee, G. H. (1999). Reflection is at the heart of practice. *Educational Leadership, 56*(8), 34–37.

Hollins, E. R. (1995). Revealing the deep meaning of culture in school learning: Framing a new paradigm for teacher preparation. *Action in Teacher Education, 27*(1), 70–79.

Honig, A. S. (1993). Mental health for babies: What do theory and research teach us? *Young Children, 48*(3), 69–76.

Honig, A. S. (1996). *Behavior guidance for infants and toddlers.* Little Rock, AR: Southern Early Childhood Association.

Hudson, P., Miller, S., Salzberg, C., & Morgan, R. (1994). The role of peer coaching in teacher education programs. *Teacher Education and Special Education, 17,* 224–235.

Humphryes, J. (1998). The developmental appropriateness of high-quality Montessori programs. *Young Children, 53*(4), 4–16.

Hunt, R. (1999). Making positive multicultural early childhood education happen. *Young Children, 54*(5), 39–42.

Hyson, M. (2002). Three perspectives on early childhood assessment. *Young Children, 57*(1), 62–64.

Jackson, B. R. (1997). Creating a climate for healing in a violent society. *Young Children, 52*(7), 68–70.

Jerald, C. (2003). Beyond the rock and the hard place. *Educational Leadership, 61*(3), 12–16.

Jones, E., & Nimmo, J. (1999). Collaboration, conflict, and change: Thoughts on education as provocation. *Young Children, 54*(1), 5–10.

Jones, J. (2004). Framing the assessment discussion. *Young Children, 59*(1), 14–18.

Jones, V. (1996). Classroom management. In J. Sikula (Ed.), *Handbook of research on teacher education* (2nd ed., pp 503–521). New York: Macmillan.

Jones, V. & Jones, L. (1986). *Comprehensive classroom management* (2nd ed.). Boston: Allyn & Bacon.

Jones, V., & Jones, L. (2004). *Comprehensive classroom management* (7th ed.). Boston: Allyn & Bacon.

Joyce, B., Hrycauk, M., Calhoun, E. et al. (2003). Learning to read in kindergarten: Has curriculum development bypassed the controversies? *Phi Delta Kappan, 85*(2), 126–132.

Kagan, S. L., & Scott-Little, C. (2004). Early learning standards: Changing the parlance and practice of early childhood education. *Phi Delta Kappan, 85*(5), 388–396.

Kampwirth, T. J. (2003). *Collaborative consultation in the schools. Effective practices for students with learning and behavior problems* (2nd ed.). Upper Saddle River, NJ: Prentice Hall.

Katz, L. G. (1994). *The project approach.* Champaign, IL: ERIC Clearinghouse on Elementary and Early Childhood Education.

Kendall, J. S. (2003). Setting standards in early childhood education. *Educational Leadership, 60*(7), 64–68.

Kilbane, C., & McNergney, R. (1999). Digital teaching portfolios build, display talent. *AACTE Briefs, 20* (13), 6.

Killoran, J., Templeman, T. P., Peters, J., & Udell, T. (2001). Identifying paraprofessional competencies for early intervention and early childhood special education. *Teaching Exceptional Children, 34*(1), 68–73.

Knowles, J. G., & Cole, A. L. (1996). Developing practice through field experiences. In F. B. Murray (Ed.), *The teacher educator's handbook* (pp. 648–688). San Francisco: Jossey-Bass.

Kohn, A. (1996). *Beyond discipline. From compliance to community.* Alexandria, VA: Association for Supervision and Curriculum Development.

Kounin, J. (1970). *Discipline and group management in classrooms.* New York: Holt, Rinehart, & Winston.

Kratcoski, A. M., & Katz, K. B. (1998). Conversing with young language learners in the classroom. *Young Children, 53*(3), 30–33.

Krogh, S. (1995). *The integrated early childhood curriculum* (2nd ed.). New York: McGraw-Hill.

Kuebli, J. (1994). Young children's understanding of everyday emotions. *Young Children, 49*(3), 36–47.

Kyle, P. B., & Rogien, L. R. (2004). *Opportunities and options in classroom management.* Boston: Allyn & Bacon.

Ladson-Billings, G. (1994). *The dreamkeepers: Successful teachers of African American children.* San Francisco: Jossey-Bass.

Lavoie, R. (1994). Parent's guide. *Learning Disabilities and Social Skills. Last One Picked . . . First One Picked on* [Video recording]. Alexandria, VA: PBS Video.

Lecca, P. J., Quervalu, I, Nunes, J. V., & Gonzales, H. F. (1998). *Cultural competency in health, social, and human services: Directions for the twenty-first century.* New York: Garland.

Lee, F. Y. (1995). Asian parents as partners. *Young Children, 50*(3), 4–9.

Lerner, J. W., Lowenthal, B., & Egan, R. (1998). *Preschool children with special needs.* Boston: Allyn & Bacon.

Levin, D. E. (2003). When the world is a dangerous place. *Educational Leadership, 60*(7), 72–75.

Litman, M., Anderson, C., Andrican, L., Buria, B., Christy, C., Koski, B., et al. (1999). Curriculum comes from the child! A head start family child care program. *Young Children, 54*(3), 4–9.

Lyons, N. (1999). How portfolios can shape emerging practice. *Educational Leadership, 56*(8), 63–65.

Machado, J. M., & Botnarescue, H. M. (2001). *Student teaching early childhood practicum guide* (4th ed.). Albany, NY: Delmar.

Macias, J. (1987). The hidden curriculum of Papago teachers: American Indian strategies for mitigating cultural discontinuity in early school. In G. Sprindler & L. Sprindler (Eds.), *Interpretive ethnography of education: At home and abroad* (pp. 363–380). Hillsdale, NJ: Lawrence Erlbaum Associates.

Madsen, C. H., & Madsen, C. R. (1974). *Teaching discipline: Behavior principles towards a positive approach.* Boston: Allyn & Bacon.

Male, M. (2003). *Technology for inclusion.* Boston: Allyn & Bacon.

Marion, M. (2003). *Guidance of young children* (6th ed.). Upper Saddle River, NJ: Merrill/Prentice Hall.

Marshall, P. L. (2002). *Cultural diversity in our schools.* Belmont, CA: Wadsworth/Thomson Learning.

Martin, G., & Pear, J. (1999). *Behavior modification. What it is and how to do it* (6th ed.). Upper Saddle River, NJ: Merrill Prentice Hall.

Martin, J. N., & Nakayama, T. K. (2000). *Intercultural communication in contexts* (2nd ed.). Mountain View, CA: Mayfield Publishing.

Martin, J. N., & Nakayama, T. K. (2005). *Experiencing intercultural communication. An introduction* (2nd ed.). Boston: McGraw-Hill.

Martin, L. A., Chiodo, J. J., & Chang, L. H. (2001). First year teachers: Looking back after three years. *Action in Teacher Education, 23*(1), 55–63.

Maxwell, K. L., & Clifford, R. M. (2004). School readiness assessment. *Young Children, 59*(1), 42–46.

Mayberry, R. I. (1994). The importance of childhood to language acquisition: Evidence from American Sign Language. In J. C. Goodman & H. C. Nusbaum (Eds.), *The development of speech perception: The transition from speech sounds to spoken words* (pp. 57–90). Cambridge, MA: MIT Press.

McAllister, P. (2003, April). *The praxis series: Meeting the "highly qualified teacher" challenge.* Testimony presented before the New Hampshire Senate Education Committee, Concord, NH.

McCarty, T. L., Lynch, R. H., Wallace, S., & Benally, A. (1991). Classroom inquiry and Navajo learning styles: A call for reassessment. *Anthropology and Education Quarterly, 22*, 42–59.

McClurg, L. G. (1998). Building an ethical community in the classroom: Community meeting. *Young Children, 53*(2), 30–38.

McEwan, E. K. (2001). *10 traits of highly effective teachers.* Thousand Oaks, CA: Corwin Press.

McIntyre, D. J., & Byrd, D. M. (1998). Supervision in teacher education. In G. R. Firth & E. F. Pajak (Eds.), *Handbook of research on school supervision* (pp. 409–427). New York: Macmillan.

McLaughlin, H. (1991). Reconciling care and control: Authority in classroom relationships. *Journal of Teacher Education, 42*(3), 182–195.

McMullen, M. B. (1999). Achieving best practices in infant and toddler care and education. *Young Children, 54*(4), 69–76.

Miller, P. C., & Endo, H. (2004). Understanding and meeting the needs of ESL students. *Phi Delta Kappan, 85*(10), 786–791.

Mindes, G. (2003). *Assessing young children* (2nd ed.). Upper Saddle River, NJ: Merrill/Prentice Hall.

Moll, L. C. (1986). Writing as communication: Creating strategic learning environments for students. *Theory into Practice, 25*(2), 102–108.

Montessori, M. (1967). *The absorbent mind* (C. A. Claremont, Trans.). New York: Holt, Rinehart, and Winston.

Morris, J. E., & Morris, G. W. (1980). Stress in student teaching. *Action in Teacher Education, 2*(4), 57–62.

Morrison, G. S. (2000). *Fundamentals of early childhood education* (2nd Ed.). Upper Saddle River, NJ: Merrill/Prentice Hall.

Morrison, T. (1998). Home. In W. Lubiano (Ed.), *The house that race built.* New York: Vintage Books.

Mulligan, S. A. (2003). Assistive technology. Suggesting the participation of children with disabilities. *Young Children, 58*(6), 50–53.

Murphy, K. L., DePasquale, R., & McNamara, E. (2003). Meaningful connections: Using technology in primary classrooms. *Young Children, 58*(6), 12–18.

NAEYC. (1998). *Helping children learn self-control: A guide to discipline.* Washington, DC: Author. Brochure.

NAEYC. (2001a). *Financing the early childhood education system.* Washington, DC: Author. Policy brief.

NAEYC. (2001b). *NAEYC standards for early childhood professional preparation.* Washington, DC: Author.

NAEYC & NAECS/SDE (National Association of Early Childhood Specialists in State Departments of Education). (2003). *Early Childhood curriculum, assessment, and program evaluation.* Joint Position Statement. Washington, DC: Author.

NAEYC & NAECS/SDE. (2002). *Early learning standards: Creating the conditions for success* [Online]. Available: *http://www.naeyc.org/resources_statements/earlylearn .pdf.*

NASDTEC. 2002. *The NASDTEC interstate contract, 2002–2005.* Mashpoe, MA: Author.

Nelson, J., Erwin, C., & Duffy, R. (1998a). *Positive discipline for preschoolers* (2nd ed.). Roseville, CA: Prima Publishing.

Nelson, J., Erwin, C., & Duffy, R. (1998b). *Positive discipline. The first three years.* Roseville, CA: Prima Publishing.

Newcomer, P. (2003). *Understanding and teaching emotionally disturbed children and adolescents.* Austin, TX: Pro-ed.

Nicholson, S., & Shipstead, S. G. (2002). *Through the looking glass. Observations in the early childhood classroom* (3rd ed.). Upper Saddle River, NJ: Merrill/Prentice Hall.

O'Hair, D., Friedrich, G. W., Wiemann, J. M., & Wiemann, M. O. (1995). *Competent communication.* New York: St. Martin's Press.

Olds, A. R. (1987). Designing settings for infants and toddlers. In C. Weinstein & T. David (Eds.), *Spaces for children: The built environment and child development.* New York: Plenum.

Olsen, G., & Fuller, M. L. (2003). *Home-school relation. Working successfully with parents and families* (2nd ed.). Boston: Allyn & Bacon.

Olsen, G., & Fuller, M. L. (1998). *Home-school relation. Working successfully with parents & families.* Boston: Allyn & Bacon.

Olsen, G., & Fuller, M. L. (1998). *Home-school relations: Working successfully with parents and families.* Boston: Allyn & Bacon.

Olson, L. (2002). Starting early. *Education Week, 21*(17), 10–14 & 16–22.

Ornstein, A. C., & Lasley, T. J. (2000). *Strategies for effective teaching.* Boston: McGraw-Hill.

Ovando, C. J. (2001). Language diversity and education. In Banks, J. A. & Banks, C. A. (Eds.), *Multicultural education: Issues and perspectives* (4th ed.,) (pp. 268–292). New York: John Wiley and Sons.

Painter, B. (2001). Using teaching portfolios. *Educational Leadership, 58*(5), 31–34.

Palmer, J. A. (1995). Environmental thinking in the early years: Understanding and misunderstanding of concepts related to waste management. *Environmental Education Research, 1*(1), 35–45.

Parette, H., & Petch-Hogan, B. (2000). Approaching families: Facilitating culturally/linguistically diverse family involvement. *Teaching Exceptional Children, 33*(2), 4–10.

Pavelich, B. (1992). Peer coaching within the internship (Monograph No. 10). Saskatoon, Canada: Center for School-Based Programs, University of Saskatchewan (ERIC Document Reproduction Service No. ED 354216).

Pelletier, C. M. (2004). *Strategies for successful student teaching* (2nd ed.). Boston: Allyn & Bacon.

Perkins-Gough, D. (2002). Teacher quality. *Educational Leadership, 60*(1), 85–86.

Piaget, J. (1963) (orig. French, 1947). *The psychology of intelligence.* Totowa, NJ: Littlefield Adams.

Piaget, J. (1971). *The construction of reality in the child.* New York: Ballantine.

Pickett, A. L. (1999). *Strengthening and supporting teacher/provider-paraprofessional teams: Guidelines for paraeducator roles, supervision, and preparation.* New York: City University of New York.

Piland, D. E., & Anglin, J. M. (1993). It is only a stage they are going through: The development of student teachers. *Action in Teacher Education, 15*(3), 19–26.

Porter, L. (1999). *Young children's behavior.* Philadelphia: MacLennan & Petty Pty Limited.

Poulson, M. K. (1993). Strategies for building resilience in infants and young children at risk. *Infants and Young Children, 6*(2), 29–40.

Pugach, M. C., & Johnson, L. J. (1995). *Collaborative practitioners, collaborative schools.* Denver, CO: Love Publishing Company.

Rauch, K., Whittaker, C. R. (1999). Observation and feedback during student teaching: Learning from peers. *Action in Teacher Education, 21*(3), 67–78.

Raver, C. C., & Zigler, E. F. (2004). Another step back? Assessing readiness in Head Start. *Young Children, 59*(1), 58–63.

Reinsberg, J. (1999). Understanding young children's behavior. *Young Children, 54*(4), 54–57.

Richards, D. D., & Siegler, R. S. (1986). Children's understandings of the attributes of life. *Journal of Experimental Child Psychology, 42,* 1–22.

Richert, A. E. (1992). Voice and power in teaching and learning to teach. In L. Valli (ed.), *Reflective Teacher Education: Cases and Critiques.* Albany: State University of New York Press.

Robinson, L. (2003). Technology as a scaffold for emergent literacy. Interactive storybooks for toddlers. *Young Children, 58*(6), 42–48.

Rodgers, D., & Dunn, M. (2000). Communication, collaboration, and complexity: Personal theory building in context. *Journal of Early Childhood Teachers Education;* 21(2): 273–280.

Roe, B. D., & Ross, E. P. (2002). *Student teaching and field experiences handbook* (5th. Ed.). Upper Saddle River, NJ: Merrill/Prentice Hall.

Rogers, C., & Freiberg, H. J. (1994). *Freedom to learn* (3rd ed.). Upper Saddle River, NJ: Merrill/Prentice Hall.

Rosenberg, M. S., O'Shea, L., & O'Shea, D. (1998). *Student teacher to master teacher.* Upper Saddle River, NJ: Merrill.

Rousseau, J. J. (1969). *Emile* (B. Foxley, Trans.). New York: Dutton. (Original work published in 1762)

Ryan, J., & Kuhs, T. (1993). Assessment of preservice teachers and the use of portfolios. *Theory Into Practice, 32,* 75–81.

Sadker, D., & Sadker, M. (1994). *Failing at fairness: How our schools cheat girls.* New York: Simon & Schuster.

Salvia, J., & Ysseldyke, J. (2004). *Assessment in special and inclusive education* (9th ed.). Boston: Houghton Mifflin.

Sandholtz, J., Ringstaff, C., & Dwyer, D. (1997). *Teaching with technology: Creating student-centered classrooms.* New York: Teachers College Press.

Santrock, J. W. (2003). *Children* (7th ed.). Columbus, OH: McGraw-Hill.

Sarbaugh, L. (1998). A taxonomic approach to intercultural communication. In Young Yan Kim & William B. Gudykunst (Eds.), *Theories in intercultural communication* (pp. 22–38). Newbury Park, CA: Sage.

Schirrmacher, R. (2002). Art and creative development for young children. (4th ed.). Albany, NY: Delmar.

Schon, D. (1983). *The reflective practitioner.* New York: Basic Books.

Schon, D. A. (1983). *The reflective practitioner: How professionals think in action.* San Francisco: Jossey-Bass.

Schwartz, S. E., & Conley, C. A. (2000). *Human diversity: A guide for understanding* (4th ed.). New York: McGraw-Hill.

Schwebel, A. I., Schwebel, B. L., Schwebel, C. R., & Schwebel, M. (1996). *The student teacher's handbook* (3rd ed.). Mahwah, NJ: Lawrence Erlbaum Associates.

Shanker, U. (1994). Protector or prison guard? Using metaphors and media to explore student teachers' thinking about classroom management. *Action in Teacher Education, 16*(1), 41–54.

Sheerer, M. A., & Bloom, P. J. (1998). Supervision in early childhood education. In G. R. Firth & E. F. Pajak (Eds.), *Handbook of research on school supervision* (pp. 581–590). New York: Macmillan Library Reference USA.

Shepard, L., Kagan, S. L., & Wurtz, E. (1998). *Principles and recommendations for early childhood assessments.* Washington, DC: National Education Goals Panel. Online: *www.negp.gov/reports/prinrec.pdf.*

Sherbet, S. (2000). Portfolios for the educator's job search. In *2000 Job search handbook for educators.* (pp. 22–23). Columbus, OH: American Association for Employment in Education.

Shore, R. (1997). *Rethinking the brain: New insights into early development.* New York: Families and Work Institute.

Shulman, L. (1998). Teacher portfolios. In N. Lyons (Ed.), *With portfolio in hand: Validating the new teacher professionalism.* New York: Teachers College Press.

Slavin, R. E. (2000). *Educational psychology* (6th ed.). Boston: Allyn & Bacon.

Slavin, R. E. (2003). *Educational psychology* (7th Ed.). Boston: Allyn & Bacon.

Smelser, N. J., Wilson, W. J., & Mitchell, F. (Eds.). (2001). *America becoming: Racial trends and their consequences* (Vols. 1–2). Washington, DC: National Academy Press.

Smith, D. J., & Sanche, R. P. (1993). Interns' personally expressed concerns: A need to extend the Fuller model. *Action in Teacher Education, 15*(3), 36–41.

Smith, P. L., Harris, C. M., Sammons, L., Waters, J., Jordan, D., Martin, D., et al. (2001). Using multimedia portfolios to assess preservice teacher and P-12 student learning. *Action in Teacher Education, 22*(4), 28–36.

Soundy, C. S., & Stout, N. L. (2002). Fostering the emotional and language needs of young learners. *Young Children, 57*(2), 21–24.

Stodolsky, S. (1985). Teacher evaluation: The limits of looking. *Educational Research, 13*(9), 11–18.

Styles, D. (2001). *Class meetings: Building leadership, problem-solving and decision-making skills in the respectful classroom.* Markham, ON: Pembroke Publishers.

Sudzina, M., Giebelhaus, C., & Coolican, M. (1997, Winter). Mentor or tormentor: The role of the cooperating teacher in student teacher success or failure. *Action in Teacher Education, xviii*(4), 23–35.

Sue, D. W. (1990). Culture-specific strategies in counseling: A conceptual framework. *Professional Psychology: Research and Practice, 21*(6), 424–433.

Tabors, P. O. (1998). What early childhood educators need to know: Developing effective programs for linguistically and culturally diverse children and families. *Young Children, 53*(6), 20–26.

Taylor, J. A., & Baker, R. A. (2001/2002). Discipline and the special education student. *Educational Leadership, 59*(4), 28–30.

Thomas, C. C., Correa, V. I., & Morsink, C. V. (2001). *Interactive teaming* (3rd ed.). Upper Saddle River, NJ: Merrill/Prentice Hall.

Toro, J. A., & Newell, E. A. (2001, August). *Professional Portfolios.* Paper presented at the meeting of The Association of Teacher Educators, Portland, OR.

TransAct Communications, Inc. (2003). *Why TransAct?* [Online]. Available: *http://www.transact.com/default .cfm?level=1,2,23*

Trawick-Smith, J. (2003). *Early childhood development. A multicultural perspective* (3rd ed.). Upper Saddle River, NJ: Merrill/Prentice Hall.

Turner, S. B. (2000). Caretaking of children's souls. Teaching the deep song. *Young Children, 55*(1), 31–33.

Tyminski, C. R. (1995). Effects of an intergenerational service-learning curriculum on refugee/immigrant students (doctoral dissertation, Temple University, 1995). *Dissertation Abstracts International,* UMI No. 9535815.

U.S. Census Bureau. (2000). *Statistical abstracts of the United States: 2000* (120th ed.). Washington, DC: Author.

U.S. Department of Education, National Center for Education Statistics (1997). *Characteristics of stayers, movers and leavers: Results from the teacher follow-up survey: 1994–95.* Washington, DC: Author.

Valdez, A. (1999). *Learning in living color.* Boston: Allyn & Bacon.

Valli, L. (1992). Beginning teacher problems: Areas for teacher education improvement. *Action in Teacher Education, 14*(1), 18–25.

Venn, J. J. (2004). *Assessing students with special needs* (3rd ed.). Upper Saddle River, NJ: Merrill/Prentice Hall.

Vygotsky, L. S. (1978). *Mind in society: The development of higher psychological processes.* Cambridge, MA: Harvard University Press.

Wadsworth, B. J. (1979). *Piaget's theory of cognitive development* (2nd ed.). New York: Longman.

Warner, L., & Sower, J. C (2005). *Educating young children from preschool through primary grades.* Boston: Allyn & Bacon.

Weaver, R. H. (2002). The roots of quality care. *Young Children, 57*(1), 16–22.

Weinstein, C. S., Woolfolk, A. E., Dittmeier, L., &

West, J. F., & Cannon, G, S. (1988). Essential collaborative consultation competencies for regular and special educators. *Journal of Learning Disabilities, 21*(1), 56–63, 28.

Westling, D. L., & Fox, L. (2000). *Teaching students with severe disabilities* (2nd Ed.). Upper Saddle River, NJ: Prentice Hall.

Wheeler, P. H. (1996). Using portfolios to assess teacher performance. In K. Burke (Ed.), *Professional portfolios: A collection of articles* (pp. 75–94). Arlington Heights, IL: IRI/Skylight Training and Publishing, Inc.

Whitebook, M., Sakai, L., Gerber, E., & Howes, C. (2001). *Then and now: Changes in childcare staffing, 1994–2000.* Washington, DC: Center for the Childcare Workforce.

Whitehead, A. N. (1929). *The aims of education.* New York: Mentor.

Whitehead, L. C., & Ginsberg, S. I. (1999). Creating a family-like atmosphere in childcare settings: All the more difficult in large childcare centers. *Young Children, 54*(2), 4–10.

Wiedmer, T. L. (1998). Digital portfolios: Capturing and demonstrating skills and levels of performance. *Phi Delta Kappan, 79*(8), 586–589.

Williams, F. (1989). *The new communications.* Belmont, CA: Wadsworth.

Wilson, R. A. (2000). Developmentally appropriate interpretation with preschool children. In M. A. Jensen & M. A. Hannibal (Eds.), *Issues, advocacy, and leadership in early education* (2nd ed.) (pp. 166–169). Boston: Allyn & Bacon. (Reprinted from *Legacy, 7*(1), 31–33, 1996, National Association for Interpretation)

Wink, J., & Putney, L. G. (2002). *A vision of Vygotsky.* Boston: Allyn & Bacon.

Wolf, K. (1996). Developing an effective teaching portfolio. *Educational Leadership, 53*(6), 34–37.

Wolf, K., Whinery, B., & Hagerty, P. (1995). Teaching portfolios and portfolio conversations for teacher educators and teachers. *Action in Teacher Education, 17*(1), 30–39.

Wolfe, P., & Brandt, R. (1998). What do we know from brain research? *Educational Leadership, 56*(3), 8–13.

Wong, Fillmiere, L. (1992). When learning a second language means losing the first. *Early Childhood Research Quarterly, 6*(3), 323–346.

Woolley, J. D. (1997). Thinking about fantasy: Are children fundamentally different thinkers and believers from adults? *Child Development, 68,* 991–1011.

Workman, S., & Anziano, M. (1993). Curriculum webs: Weaving connections from children to teachers. *Young Children, 48*(2), 4–9.

Worsley, M., Beneke, S., & Helm, J. H. (2003). The pizza project: Planning and integrating math standards in project work. *Young Children, 58*(1), 44–50.

Wortham, S. C. (2002). *Early childhood curriculum* (3rd Ed.). Upper Saddle River, NJ: Merrill/Prentice Hall.

Yoo, S. (2001). Using portfolios to reflect on practice. *Educational Leadership, 58*(8), 78–81.

Young, L. S. J., & Edwards, P. A. (1996). Parents, families, and communities: Opportunities for preservice teacher education. In F. B. Murray (Ed.), *The teacher educator's handbook* (pp. 438–462). San Francisco: Jossey-Bass.

Zachary, L. J. (2000). *The mentor's guide.* San Francisco: Jossey-Bass.

Zeichner, K. M., & Liston, D. P. (1996). *Reflective teaching. An introduction.* Mahwah, NJ: Lawrence Erlbaum Associates.

Zellermayer, M. (2001). Resistance as a catalyst in teachers' professional development. In C. M. Clark (Ed.), *Talking shop* (pp. 40–63). New York: Teachers College Press.

Zubizarreta, J. (1994). Teaching portfolios and the beginning teacher. *Phi Delta Kappan, 76,* 323–326.

Index